Madrid's
25Best

by Jonathan Holland

Fodor's Travel Publications
New York • Toronto
London • Sydney • Auckland
www.fodors.com

How to Use This Book

KEY TO SYMBOLS

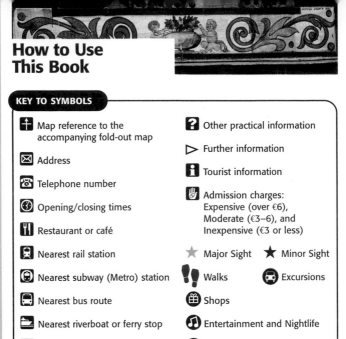

✚ Map reference to the accompanying fold-out map	❓ Other practical information
✉ Address	▷ Further information
☎ Telephone number	ℹ Tourist information
🕓 Opening/closing times	✋ Admission charges: Expensive (over €6), Moderate (€3–6), and Inexpensive (€3 or less)
🍴 Restaurant or café	
🚈 Nearest rail station	★ Major Sight ★ Minor Sight
🚇 Nearest subway (Metro) station	👣 Walks 🚌 Excursions
🚌 Nearest bus route	🏛 Shops
⛴ Nearest riverboat or ferry stop	🎵 Entertainment and Nightlife
♿ Facilities for visitors with disabilities	🍴 Restaurants

This guide is divided into four sections

• **Essential Madrid:** an introduction to the city and tips on making the most of your stay.
• **Madrid by Area:** We've broken the city into five areas, and recommended the best sights, shops, entertainment venues, nightlife and restaurants in each one. Suggested walks help you to explore on foot.
• **Where to Stay:** the best hotels, whether you're looking for luxury, budget or something in between.
• **Need to Know:** the info you need to make your trip run smoothly, including getting about by public transport, weather tips, emergency phone numbers and useful websites.

Navigation In the Madrid by Area chapter, we've given each area its own colour, which is also used on the locator maps throughout the book and the map on the inside front cover.

Maps The fold-out map accompanying this book is a comprehensive street plan of Madrid. The grid on this fold-out map is the same as the grid on the locator maps within the book. We've given grid references within the book for each sight and listing.

Contents

Introducing Madrid

In 1561, King Felipe II made Madrid capital of what soon became the world's biggest empire. Today, the grandeur remains: churches and museums, palaces and parks. But there are also medieval lanes and modern skyscrapers. That's why Madrid is unique.

Nowhere else in the world is the past so close to the present. Nuns and monks still live and worship in convents and monasteries that date back for centuries. Shops still make traditional cakes and breads; locals still stop for olives and a small glass of wine in the way that their forebears have done for centuries. But Madrid is also a city known for its exciting modern architecture, for its trendy small hotels, for its nightlife, with bars and clubs open till dawn…and even later at weekends. While thousands flock to watch the traditional rites at the world's most famous bullring, even more fans head for the Estadio Santiago Bernabéu to watch Real Madrid, arguably the most famous football club in the world.

No other city on the planet has three such high-quality museums within a few minutes' walk of each other. But Madrid has dozens of smaller museums that are less crowded and give an insight into the glory and grandeur that was imperial Spain. And it is all so walkable. Stroll around or, if your feet complain, take one of the cleanest, safest and cheapest public transport systems in the world. It is easy to get anywhere in minutes.

This is a city where you need to go with the flow. Only a foreigner eats dinner as early as nine at night; only a foreigner walks the boiling pavements on an afternoon in high summer; only a foreigner spends a whole evening at the same tapas bar. So do as locals do: try different tapas at different bars, sit down to dinner at 10pm, take an afternoon nap, then stay up to the small hours.

Facts + Figures

- The population of Madrid is 3.2 million.
- Madrid is Europe's third largest city, after London and Berlin.
- Madrid is the highest capital in Europe (646m/2,120ft).

SIMPLY THE BEST

FIFA, football's world governing body, recognized Real Madrid as the world's best football club of the 20th century. You can tour their stadium, named for their former president, Santiago Bernabéu. He put up the idea of the Intercontinental Cup, a match between the champions of Europe and the champions of South America.

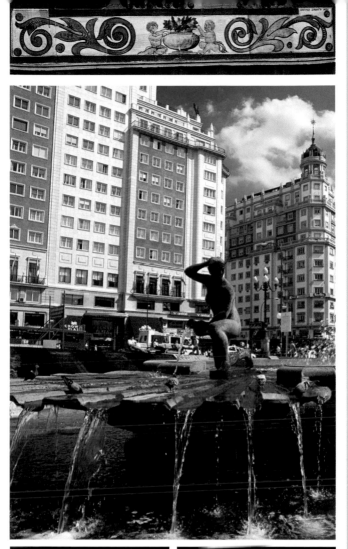

LUCKY GRAPES

Everyone in Spain recognizes the clock on the Casa de Correos in the Puerta del Sol. It is used to welcome the New Year at midnight. For each of the 12 tolls of the bell, Spaniards, in the plaza and watching TV across the country, eat a grape for good luck: *uvas de la suerte*.

MOVIE MAGIC

Pedro Almodóvar set several films in Madrid. *Laberinto de Pasiones* (1982) was shot at the Rastro Sunday market, where he once had a stand; Pénelope Cruz appeared in *Plaza Mayor in Flor de mi Secreto* (1995); and part of *Tacones Lejanos* (1991) was shot in the Villa Rosa night club.

5

A Short Stay in Madrid

DAY 1

Morning To beat the crowds in the city's three great museums, you need a prompt start. For the **Museo Nacional Reina Sofía** (▷ 47), use the new extension entrance to the museum (off the Glorieta de Carlos V), still undiscovered by the main rush. Go straight up to see Picasso's *Guernica*, then work your way down.

Lunch Once the crowds build up at the museum, take the Metro across to Serrano for a smart lunch at **Sula** (▷ 80) or any of the myriad cafés.

Afternoon Now hit the shops. Work your way up Serrano to the **ABC Serrano** (▷ 92), a gallery of smart boutiques. Stroll down the streets called Goya, Velázquez and Ortega y Gasset. Then go back to your hotel for a siesta.

Evening Linger over tapas in the bars on and around the Plaza de Santa Ana. As well as traditional haunts, such as the Cervecería Alemana, there are contemporary wine bars, such as the **Vinoteca Barbechera** (▷ 66). Stroll down to the **Museo Thyssen-Bornemisza** (▷ 48) and soak up some culture. In July and August, the museum stays open late during 'Noches de verano', Summer Nights.

Dinner Afterwards, still in the Museo Thyssen-Bornemisza, dine at the **El Mirador del Museo restaurant**, on the terrace, high above the city.

Later The Spanish love to stay up late, late, late. Hit a popular club such as the **Café Central** (▷ 63) for jazz or the **Casa Patas** (▷ 63) for flamenco. And if you are still going strong at 4am, join the locals at **Chocolatería San Ginés** (▷ 65) for hot chocolate before heading for bed.

Morning If it is a Sunday morning, then do what everyone does: go to El Rastro (▷ 53). This swirling mix of outdoor markets and shops has everything from cheap toys, pottery and clothing to expensive antiques and leather goods. Make sure that you have no visible or tempting handbag or wallet on view. Afterwards, drift through the narrow lanes towards the **Plaza de Tirso de Molina**, with its cheerful flower stands, smart new paving, fountains and statue of Tirso de Molina himself. The real name of this playwright was Gabriel Tellez, and he is best remembered for his character, Don Juan. Stroll on east through the old city streets and join locals grazing along Calle de Jésus at tapas bars such as **Cervecería Cervantes** (▷ 65).

Lunch Instead of a big meal, continue hopping in and out of the line of tapas bars along the street. Have dessert at La Esquina del Café (▷ 65).

Afternoon Cross the Paseo del Prado and watch *madrileños* at play in the **Retiro Park** (▷ 75). Puppet shows for little children; boats for hire on the lake; live concerts in summer, when most are happy to stretch out on the lawns and snooze.

Evening Another authentic Madrid experience is the *zarzuela*. Part Gilbert & Sullivan, part Feydeau farce, these are Spanish comic operas. The music is jolly, the plots are silly, so you don't need to understand the language. The **Teatro de la Zarzuela** (▷ 64) also stages ballet and dance.

Dinner To keep the Spanish experience going, dine nearby at **Taberna Maceira** (▷ 66), where crowds pack in elbow-to-elbow at wooden tables for simple, hearty, Galician dishes.

Top 25

▶ ▶ ▶

Casa de Campo ▷ 24
Take a break from the art-works in Madrid's vast 'green lung'.

Catedral de la Almudena ▷ 25 Madrid's most important church has an impressive clifftop setting.

Ermita de San Antonio ▷ 26 Superb Goya frescoes adorn the chapel where he is buried.

El Rastro ▷ 53 For bargains galore, the legendary Sunday market still attracts locals and visitors alike.

Real Madrid ▷ 100
Spain's most illustrious football club has its home at the impressive Santiago Bernabéu stadium.

Real Academia de Bellas Artes ▷ 54–55 The Fine Arts Academy is best known for its Goya self-portraits.

Puerta del Sol ▷ 52 The 'gateway of the sun' has been the heart of the city since the 15th century.

Puerta de Alcalá ▷ 75
The neoclassical gateway to Madrid is dramatically lit at night.

Plaza de Toros ▷ 98 Its sheer scale makes the bullring impressive, even if you don't come to watch a fight.

Plaza de Oriente ▷ 35
Elegant, pedestrianized square that is a welcome haven of peace in the city.

Plaza Mayor ▷ 51
Madrid's handsomest square, famous for its fres-coed Casa de la Panadería.

Plaza de la Cibeles ▷ 74 The Cibeles Fountain is the city's best-loved landmark.

These pages are a quick guide to the Top 25, which are described in more detail later. Here they are listed alphabetically, and the tinted background shows which area they are in.

Monasterio de las Descalzas Reales ▷ 50
16th-century convent that is a treasure house of artwork.

Monasterio de la Encarnación ▷ 27
Former convent famous for its reliquaries.

Museo de América ▷ 30 Outstanding museum dedicated to the art and culture of the Americas.

Museo Cerralbo ▷ 28–29 The home and artworks of a 19th-century marquis.

Museo Lázaro Galdiano ▷ 84–85 Eclectic collection of *objets d'art*.

Museo Nacional Reina Sofía ▷ 46–47 Spain's national museum of modern art.

Museo del Prado ▷ 70–71 Madrid's biggest visitor attraction, this incomparable collection contains more than 8,000 paintings.

Museo Sorolla ▷ 86–87 Museum dedicated to the the life and works of 'the Spanish impressionist'.

Museo Thyssen-Bornemisza ▷ 48–49 One of the finest privately amassed art collections.

Museo del Traje ▷ 31 Dress up in 18th-century clothing at Madrid's most exciting new museum.

Parque del Retiro ▷ 72–73 Enjoy the shady paths and formal gardens of Madrid's central park.

Parque del Oeste ▷ 34 Madrid's most attractive green space is ideal for a summer stroll.

Palacio Real ▷ 32–33 The vast 18th-century Royal Palace is an outstanding historical monument.

◄ ◄ ◄

Shopping

Since the 1980s, out-of-town malls have sprung up and international chains have crept in. But fears that late 20th-century shopping practices would kill off Madrid's many unique little stores have been largely unfounded, and the range of shopping experiences available for visitors is wonderfully diverse. It's these contrasts between the best on the international scene with some superbly idiosyncratic outlets that make Madrid shopping so serendipitous.

A Bit of Everything
It's not just what shops sell that provides a contrast—how they look is also varied. Temples of consumerism in steel and glass happily rub shoulders with cramped, dark shops where the stock is piled high and the merchandise specialized beyond belief. Few other world capitals have as many stores devoted to so many oddities—outsize corsetry, plaster statuary, crystallized violets. This gives Madrid shopping a special appeal, whether you're after easy-to-carry souvenirs or seriously self-indulgent retail therapy, or you simply enjoy window-shopping.

Clothes and Accessories
Madrid has branches of some of Spain and Europe's best-known fashion stores, as well as

Flamenco shop; designer store; flea market; legs of ham (top to bottom)

WHERE TO SHOP

Ask a *madrileño* where to find the city's shopping heart and the answer is bound to be around Calle Preciados, the pedestrianized drag that connects Puerta del Sol with the Gran Vía. Here you'll find branches of all the big chain stores, as well as Madrid's biggest department store, and everything from fashion to food. Smarter by far are the quiet, well-heeled streets of the Salamanca district, home to the big designer names and luxury stores of all description. The best places to trawl for souvenirs are around the Plaza Mayor and the surrounding Los Austrias district, or Malasaña. Head for Chueca for cutting-edge style and street fashion.

the latest in the stylish, chain-store fashion, for which Spain is renowned. Spanish leather shoes, bags and belts are some of the best in Europe, and excellent value.

Gifts

For gifts, you'll find goods from all over Spain, ranging from the tasteful fringed and embroidered shawls and *mantillas*, warm winter capes, elegant hats, delicate china, traditional ceramics and damascene work, to the marvellously tacky (plastic flamenco dolls, a poster of a *torero* with your name on it and metal Don Quixotes).

Food

Food makes a great souvenir or gift. In addition to the obvious olive oil, nougat or chocolate, hunt down saffron, wonderful dried nuts, seeds and the fruits so loved by the Spanish. Or look for convent-baked biscuits or cakes, vacuum-packed *jamón* (dry-cured ham), *chorizo* (spicy sausage) or *morcilla* (unctuous black pudding).

Tax Refunds and Sales

IVA (sales tax) is added at 7 per cent on food and 16 per cent on most other items. Non-EU visitors can reclaim the IVA on purchases, but the total must be at least €90.15, paid in a single store in a single day. Stores taking part display a Tax-Free shopping sticker. For more detailed information, see www.okspain.org. Sales generally run from mid-January to February, and July to August.

Flea market; lace fans; shop window (top to bottom)

MARKETS

Markets are not only a window into everyday life, but also the perfect place to pick up a picnic to eat in the park. Some of the best are La Cebada (🚇 La Latina)–for a huge range of goods and low prices; El Rastro (🚇 La Latina)–the famous Sunday market; and La Paz (🚇 Serrano)–quality and varied produce aimed at the prosperous Salamanca inhabitants.

Shopping by Theme

Whether you're looking for a department store, a quirky boutique, or something in between, you'll find it all in Madrid. On this page shops are listed by theme. For a more detailed write-up, see the individual listings in Madrid by Area.

Madori by Night

Madrid has a year-round agenda of cultural evening events, from opera, orchestral concerts, plays, dance and original-language films to jazz, flamenco and Latin American music. Get information in the weekly entertainment guide *Guía del Ocio* or the monthly English-language *InMadrid* (see below), and reserve tickets for concerts and plays via www.entradas.com (☎ 90 222 16 22) or Localidades Galicia (☎ 91 531 27 32; www.eol.es/lgalicia) ticket lines.

A Quiet Evening

With little hope of a restaurant dinner before 9, you might want to take your evening stroll before you eat. Touristy though it is, the Plaza Mayor looks great by night; from here you can wander through buzzing Huertas down to the wide Paseo del Prado, a wonderful place in summer for a stroll and a drink at a *terraza*. A few minutes' walk away lies the Retiro Park, perfect on balmy evenings. For window shopping, head for the elegant streets of Salamanca or Chueca.

Night Owls

Madrid's reputation as an all-night party town is deserved. Check out what's what in the free English-language listings magazines, *InMadrid* or *The Broadsheet*. Nightlife concentrates around Huertas, Lavapiés, Malasaña and off Sol. Gay-oriented Chueca is ultra cool and Salamanca is for a dressed-up occasion.

FLOODLIT STONE

Great cities look wonderful under floodlights and Madrid is no exception. Imaginative lighting enhances much of the city after dark. Don't miss the subtly lit charms of the Plaza Mayor, then enjoy the brilliance lighting adds to the Palacio Real and the Plaza de Oriente. The Paseo del Prado is beautifully illuminated at night; admire the sparkle of light on the water of the fountains in Plaza de Cibeles and Plaza de Canovas de Castillo before stopping at one of the summertime *terrazas*.

Flamenco show; musicians performing; flamenco dancer; taberna sign (top to bottom)

Eating Out

You can eat regional food from all over the peninsula in Madrid, as well as superb tapas, snacks and dishes from farther afield.

Where to Eat

There's a huge choice of eating places in Madrid, particularly around Sol, Santa Ana and Huertas, and the Latina, Lavapiés, Chueca and Malasaña districts. The city's smartest and priciest restaurants are concentrated near the Paseo del Prado and the Retiro and scattered throughout Salamanca. The IVA tax of 7 per cent is added to bills in restaurants and bars. As for tipping, service is included; however it is customary to leave a few coins in a bar and 5 per cent in a restaurant.

Types of Restaurant

Restaurantes are officially graded with 1 to 5 forks, and range from simple establishments serving up the trusty *menú del día* to very grand—and pricey—establishments. Tapas bars are quintessentially Spanish. These snacks range from a few olives or almonds to tortillas, shellfish, meat croquettes and wonderful vegetable dishes laced with garlic. All tapas bars have their own special dishes, and locals move from place to place, ordering the dishes that each bar does particularly well. The barman normally keeps track of what you've had to eat, and you pay at the end. The city has a very active café life, with some wonderful old places where you can read the papers and watch the world go by.

MEAL TIMES

The Spanish usually eat breakfast (*desayuno*) between 9 and 10, though it is served earlier in hotels. It's usually sweet—*chocolate con churros* (hot chocolate and stick-shaped doughnuts) or toast with jam. Traditionally, the main meal of the day, lunch (*almuerzo*) is from 2 to 4. The Spanish eat dinner (*cena*) any time after 9.30 through till midnight. But, with cafés and tapas bars open long hours, you can always find something tasty to eat.

Tapas bar; pinchos; *taberna;* tapas dishes *(top to bottom)*

Restaurants by Cuisine

There are restaurants to suit all tastes and budgets in Madrid. On this page they are listed by cuisine. For a more detailed description of each restaurant, see Madrid by Area.

BASQUE AND CATALAN

Bokado (▷ 41)
Dantxari (▷ 41)
Errota-Zar (▷ 65)

COFFEE, TEA, CHOCOLATE AND ICE CREAM

Bajo Cero (▷ 94)
Chocolatería San Ginés (▷ 65)
La Esquina del Café (▷ 65)
Ritz Hotel (▷ 80)

GALICIAN AND ASTURIAN

A'Casiña (▷ 41)
Casa Mingo (▷ 41)
La Hoja (▷ 80)
Restaurante Moaña (▷ 66)
Taberna Maceira (▷ 66)

NATIONAL AND INTERNATIONAL

AC Palacio del Retiro (▷ 79)
El 4 de Tapas (▷ 94)
Balzac (▷ 79)
La Castela (▷ 79)
La Gamella (▷ 80)

Nina Madrid (▷ 94)
Pedro Larumbe (▷ 94)
El Placer del Espíritu Santo (▷ 94)
Restaurante Viridiana (▷ 80)
La Sacristía (▷ 94)
Sula (▷ 80)
La Taquería de Birra (▷ 42)
Trattoria Sant'Arcangelo (▷ 80)

SPANISH

El Ingenio (▷ 41)
Mesón Cinco Jotas (▷ 42)
Mi Pueblo (▷ 42)
Prada a Tope (▷ 42)
Sal Gorda (▷ 42)
El Senador (▷ 42)
La Taurina (▷ 66)
Viuda de Vacas (▷ 66)

TAPAS

Baztán (▷ 94)
Los Caracoles (▷ 65)
Casa Alberto (▷ 65)
Casa Labra (▷ 65)
Cervecería Cervantes (▷ 65)
Lhardy (▷ 65)
Sanlúcar (▷ 42)
Taberna de Antonio Sánchez (▷ 66)
Vinoteca Barbechera (▷ 66)

TRADITIONAL MADRID CUISINE

La Bola Taberna (▷ 41)
Botín (▷ 65)
Café de Oriente (▷ 41)
El Molino de Los Porches (▷ 42)
Posada de la Villa (▷ 66)

If You Like...

Whatever your special interest while you are in Madrid, these suggestions should help you to make the most of your visit. Each sight or listing has more details later on in the book.

PEOPLE-WATCHING

Café de Oriente (▷ 41): next to the Opera House, facing the Royal Palace.
Plaza Mayor: for architecture, murals, statues (▷ 51).
Retiro park lake: in a rowing boat (▷ 73).
Teleférico **(cable car):** on the way to or from the Campo de Moro (▷ 34).

SHOPPING TILL YOU DROP

ABC Serrano: a stylish indoor mall, with classy boutiques (▷ 92).
The Rastro: the fun Sunday morning market (▷ 53).
El Corte Inglés: Spain's top department store (▷ 61).
Mercado de Fuencarral: funky and fun (▷ 92).

Teleférico; *shopping spree (above)*

CHECKING OUT GREAT ART

The Prado: for Goya's greatest works (▷ 70).
Museo Nacional Reina Sofía: for Picasso's *Guernica* (▷ 46).
Museo Thyssen-Bornemisza: for 19th-century American art (▷ 48).

SPLASHING OUT

Genuine antiques: in the Galerías Piquér (▷ 62).
Fine ceramics: Antigua Casa Talavera (▷ 61).
A real fan: Casa de Diego (▷ 61).

The view of the Palacio de Cristál across the lake in El Retiro Park (above right); eye-catching fans (right)

Flamenco show (below)

BEING ENTERTAINED

Bullfighting: at the Plaza de Toros, the world's No.1 arena (▷ 98).

Flamenco: at a dozen clubs, such as Casa Patas (▷ 63).

Football: at Real Madrid, Atlético de Madrid, Rayo Vallecano.

Jazz: at the Café Central (▷ 63).

KEEPING KIDS HAPPY

Carriage ride: tour the city by night.

Casa de Campo: go to the Parque de Atracciones, fairground (▷ 24).

Museo del Traje: dress up in 18th-century garb (▷ 31).

Playgrounds: let off steam in renovated plazas, such as the Plaza de Santa Ana (▷ 59), Tirso de Molina.

KEEPING TO A TIGHT BUDGET

Concerts: check out free concerts in the Retiro park (▷ 73).

Festivals: ask at the tourist office if there are any parades, processions.

Free entry: visit museums on their weekly free entrance days.

Casa de Campo; flamingos in the zoo at Casa de Campo (above)

Museo De Escultura al Aire Libre: great sculpture free at the outdoor sculpture museum (▷ 89).

TRADITIONAL TAPAS

El 4 De Tapas (▷ 94).
Taberna de Antonio Sánchez (▷ 66).
Los Caracoles (▷ 65).

Selection of tapas (left)

ESSENTIAL MADRID IF YOU LIKE...

OLD-FASHIONED FEASTING

Restaurante Botín; stay in a funky hotel (below)

Botín: the world's oldest restaurant (▷ 65).
Taberna Maceira: Galician cooking, especially *pulpo* (octopus) (▷ 66).
Restaurante Moaña: fish, seafood in a formal setting (▷ 66).
Posada de la Villa: traditional Madrid oven-roast lamb (▷ 66).

FUNKY HOTELS

Hospes: a new boutique hotel in a classic building (▷ 112).
ME Madrid: was the posh old Reina Victoria, now hip and happening (▷ 112).
Petit Palace: in the swish part of town, on top of the best window-shopping around (▷ 112).
Quo: a new group of funky hotels in the city (▷ 112).

CELEB-SPOTTING

La Bardemcilla (Augusto Figueroa 47), owned by film stars Monica and Javier Bardém.
Bar Skynight, on top of the Hotel Puerta América (Avenida de América) (▷ 112).
Fortuny, once a palace, still glitzy (▷ 93).
Glass Bar at the posh Hotel Urban (▷ 64).

PARTYING TILL DAWN

Cocktails (above)

Ojalá Awareness Club: the indoor beach is a must (▷ 93).
Blue Note: jazz with a Brazilian beat (▷ 93).
Kapital: seven floors of fun at Madrid's biggest club (▷ 79).

Dancing in a club (right)

18

Madrid by Area

The Royal Palace is now a museum, but this area retains the elegance of the past. There are also plenty of green spaces.

CALLE ISAAC PERAL

Plaza Cristo Rey

P

P

CALLE DE Argüelles

Mercado La

CALLE ALBERTO AGUILERA

URQUIJO

Buen Suceso

Calle

San Francisco

Quintana

Servicio Histórico del Ejército

UNIVERSIDAD

Antiguo Cuartel del Conde Duque

Ventura Rodriguez

Plaza Cristino Martos

Calle del Rey

Calle Martin de los Heros

Templo de Debod

Calle Ferraz

Torre de Madrid

Plaza de los Reyes

Plaza España

Mon a Cervantes

GRAN

Calle del Rio

Museo Cerralbo

Plaza de España

Calle Tirso Molina

Palacio del Senado

VIA

SAN VICENTE

BAILEN

Calle de Torija

Santo Domingo

Campo del Moro

Jardines de Sabatini

Calle

Monasterio de la Encarnación

CUESTA DE

PALACIO

Palacio Real

Plaza de Oriente

de Arrieta

Plaza de la Armeria

Calle Vergara

Calle San Nicolás

Teatro Real

Opera

Catedral de la Almudena

San Nicolás de los Servitas

Plasencia

Muralla Arabe

BAILEN

Parque Emir Mohamed I

DE SEGOVIA

Viaducto

CALLE DE

Calle Beatriz Galindo

Plaza G Miró

Plaza Granado

Calle Don Pedro

Capilla Cristo de los Dolores

Plaza San Francisco

Jardines de las Vistillas

Basilica de San Francisco el Grande

CALLE SAN FRANCISCO

RONDA DE SEGOVIA

PASEO IMPERIAL

E   F   G

Casa de Campo

Flamingos in the zoo (left); running in Casa de Campo (right)

THE BASICS

✚ A6

✉ Calle Marqués de Monistrol, Avenida de Portugal

🚇 Lago, Batán, Casa de Campo

🚌 41, 33, 39, 65, 75, 84

Parque de Atracciones
www.parquedeatracciones.es

✚ Off map at A7

☎ 91 463 29 00

🕐 Jul–end Sep Mon–Thu, Sun noon–1am, Fri, Sat noon–2am; Oct–end Jun Mon–Fri noon–dusk, Sat noon–1am

🍴 Cafés, restaurants

🚇 Batán

🚌 33, 36, 39, 65

💵 Expensive

Zoo-Aquarium de Madrid
www.zoomadrid.com

✚ Off map at A7

☎ 91 512 37 70

🕐 Daily 10.30–dusk

🍴 Cafés, restaurants

🚇 Batán, Casa de Campo

🚌 33

💵 Expensive

TIP

● Take the 11-minute cable car trip from Parque del Oeste for superb views over the city.

That Madrid is one of Europe's greenest capitals is mainly because of the 1,722ha (4,255-acre) Casa de Campo, 'the lungs of Madrid', stretching away to the north-west. Once a royal hunting estate, it was opened to the public in 1931, quickly becoming popular as a cool haven in Madrid's hot summer.

Wide open space In Casa de Campo, you can walk for a couple of hours without being interrupted (though this is best avoided after dark). During the Civil War, Franco's troops were based here, and signs of trenches are still visible. The park contains sports facilities, a large lake (where you can hire boats), amusement park, aquarium and zoo. The *teleférico* (cable car, www.teleferico.com) runs up here from the Parque del Oeste (▷ 34), and the 11-minute journey is an excellent way to arrive, affording superb views over the city.

Parque de Atracciones This amusement park has more than 40 rides, from gentle merry-go-rounds to the stomach-churning Top Spin and the breathtaking Tornado rollercoaster. There are open-air concerts in summer.

The zoo Madrid's zoo is one of the best in Europe. It contains over 2,000 animals and more than 100 species of bird, including 29 endangered species. There is a dolphinarium with twice-daily shows, a train ride, an aquarium and a children's section. Parrot shows, the tank of sharks and birds of prey are all popular.

Inside (left) the neo-classical Catedral de la Almudena (middle and right)

Catedral de la Almudena

Though not the loveliest cathedral, it reflects years of Spanish architectural thought. The mixture of styles shows how relaxed *madrileños* have been about this building, which you would expect to have been a priority.

A long delay A little over a decade ago, Madrid lacked a cathedral, incredible though it may seem. The first plans for the Almudena, constructed on what was formerly the site of Muslim Madrid's principal mosque, were drawn up in 1879 under Alfonso XII by the architect Giambattista Sacchetti. Redesigned in 1883, it is based on the pattern of a 13th-century cathedral, with a chancel similar to the one at Rheims. A neoclassical style was introduced into the design in 1944, but it wasn't until 1993, when the final touches were added, that the cathedral was consecrated by the Pope. The main entrance is opposite the Royal Palace, the entrance to the crypt along La Cuesta de la Vega.

The story of the Almudena Virgin According to legend, the image of the Virgin over the entrance had been hidden in the 11th century by Mozarabs. When Spanish hero El Cid reconquered Madrid, he ordered that the image be found, but without success. Alfonso VI then instructed his troops and the people of Madrid to dismantle the city walls to find the image. When they reached the grain deposits, they heard a noise from the turrets above, which then collapsed, revealing an image of the Virgin and Child.

THE BASICS

- ⊞ E7
- ✉ Calle Bailén. Next to Palacio Real
- ☎ 91 542 22 00
- 🕐 Daily 9–9
- Ⓜ Ópera
- 🚌 3, 31, 148
- 🎟 Free
- ♿ Good

HIGHLIGHTS

- Virgin of Almudena
- Coffin of San Isidro
- Dome 20m (66ft) in diameter
- Grenzing organ
- The 104m (340ft)-long nave
- 12 statues of the apostles
- Bronze doors

Ermita de San Antonio de la Florida

The façade of the hermitage (left); the exterior (right)

www.munimadrid.es/ermita

✚ C6

✉ Glorieta de San Antonio de la Florida 5

☎ 91 542 07 22

🕐 Tue–Fri 9.30–8; Sat, Sun 10–2. Closed public hols

Ⓜ Príncipe Pío

🚍 41, 46, 75

🚉 Norte Station

♿ None

🎟 Free

HIGHLIGHTS

● Cupola
● Balustrade
● Marble and stucco font (1798)
● *Lápida de Goya*
● Mirrors under the cupola
● High altar
● Lamp under the cupola (18th century)
● *Inmaculada*, Jacinto Gómez Pastor
● *San Luis and San Isidro*, Jacinto Gómez Pastor

Goya is surely the painter that most *madrileños* want to claim as their own. The San Antonio de la Florida Hermitage, a National Monument, is a fine memorial to his memory.

Resting place Both church and hermitage—the latter to the left as you face the two buildings—are off the beaten track, but worthwhile both for their intimacy and to view Goya's frescoes. The original hermitage was begun in 1792 by Charles IV's Italian architect, Francisco Fontana. Goya's remains were buried here in 1919, but without his head: it is said that it was stolen by scientists who wished to study it.

The frescoes Painted using a technique that was revolutionary at the time, the frescoes are distinguished by their richness of colour. They tell the life of Saint Anthony, representing the saint raising a murdered man from the dead to enable him to name his murderer and spare the life of the innocent accused. The models for the frescoes were members of the Spanish Court, but include other, less reputable figures—placing rogues alongside the Court officials has been seen as indicating Goya's contempt for the Court of the time.

Girlfriends and boyfriends Saint Anthony is the patron saint of sweethearts, and every 13 June girls come here to pray for a boyfriend. Thirteen pins are placed inside the font; then a girl puts her hand in and the number of pins that stick indicates how many beaux she will have that year.

The Monastery of the Incarnation (left); St. Teresa in stained-glass (right)

Located away from the traffic of Calle Bailén, the Monastery of the Incarnation is suffused with religious calm that brings peace to the soul.

History Designed by Juan Gómez de Mora in 1611 on instructions from Queen Margarita, wife of Philip III, the church in the Royal Monastery is typical of Habsburg Spanish religious architecture. Originally the monastery was connected by a secret passage to the Arab fortress where the Royal Palace now stands. The church was damaged by fire in 1734, and reconstructed in classical baroque style; the granite façade is all that remains of the original. A 45-minute guided tour leads you through the monastery, which is still used by nuns of the Augustine order; you see the Royal Room, hung with uninspired portraits of the royal family, and one of Madrid's most beautiful churches, the monastery church, which includes a reliquary. Here, also, is the monastery museum.

The Reliquary In the middle of the church stands an altar and altarpiece depicting the Holy Family by Bernadino Luini, a pupil of Leonardo da Vinci, and an ornate tabernacle in bronze and rock crystal. Inside is a crucifix of Christ with a crown of thorns, oddly charred: tradition holds that these are the remains of a crucifix defiled by heretics. Among the 1,500 relics on display, in a small glass globe to the right of the door as you enter is the dried blood of St. Pantaleón, which mysteriously liquefies every year on 27 July, St. Pantaleón's Day.

THE BASICS

www.patrimonionacional.es

⊞ E7

✉ Plaza de la Encarnación 1

☎ 91 454 88 00

◉ Monastery and Reliquary: Tue–Thu and Sat 10.30–12.45, 4–5.45; Fri 10.30–12.45; Sun 11–1.45

Ⓜ Ópera, Santo Domingo

🚌 3, 25, 39, 148

💶 Inexpensive. Free Wed for EU citizens

♿ None

HIGHLIGHTS

● *John the Baptist*, Jusepe Ribera
● *Handing over of the Princesses*, anonymous painting in lobby
● *Recumbent Christ*, Perronius
● Royal Room
● Altarpiece
● Cupola, with frescoes by González Velázquez
● Frescoes: Francisco Bayeu
● Charred crucifix
● Blood of St. Pantaleón

Museo Cerralbo

HIGHLIGHTS

- Grand staircase
- *Ecstasy of St. Francis,* El Greco
- *Jacob with his Flock,* José de Ribera
- *Devotion,* Alonso Cano
- *Immaculate Conception,* Francisco Zurbarán
- *Porcupines and Snakes,* Frans Snyders
- Sword collection from the courts of Louis XV and XVI
- Monumental mystery clock

TIP

- Entry is free on Wednesday and Sunday till closing time (3pm).

Idiosyncratic and intermittently splendid, this curiosity shows you how the nobility of Madrid lived 100 years ago, in particular the extravagant and fascinating Marquis de Cerralbo.

Home life When you see the two-floor, late 19th-century home of the 17th Marquis of Cerralbo from the outside it looks rather unpromising. But the clutter of artefacts inside is fascinating, and uniquely among the house-museums in Madrid, the collections are rivalled by the architecture and décor of the rooms themselves, ranging from the frankly shabby to the magnificent. Politician, man of letters and collector, the Marquis donated the house and its contents to the state in 1922, stipulating that his collection be displayed exactly as he had left it. This is a unique

The grand staircase (left); the mirrored ballroom (right)

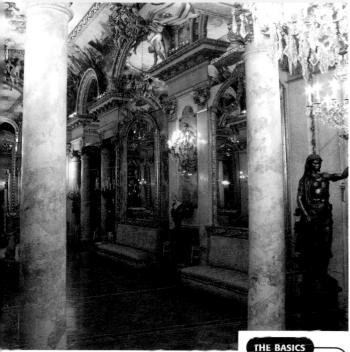

opportunity to see a near-intact aristocrat's home of the turn of the 20th century.

The collection A magnificent grand staircase by Soriano Fort is to your right as you enter. On the second floor, the most notable exhibit is El Greco's striking *Ecstasy of St. Francis* (1600–05) in the chapel. In the gallery surrounding the patio, there are works by José de Ribera and Alonso Cano, as well as haunting Alessandro Magnasco landscapes. On the third floor there are collections of Western and oriental weaponry, a dining room containing a remarkable Frans Snyders painting, and an appealingly homey library. Pride of place is given to the sumptuous mirrored ballroom on the first floor, which displays the Marquis' Saxon porcelain, as well as intricate clocks, including one particularly fascinating and huge specimen.

THE BASICS

http://museocerralbo.
mcu.es
✚ E6
✉ Calle Ventura
Rodríguez 17
☎ 91 547 36 46
🕐 Jul–Aug Tue–Sat
9.30–2, Sun 10–2; Sep–Jun
Tue–Sat 9.30–3, Sun 10–3.
Tours in Spanish only
🚇 Ventura Rodríguez,
Plaza de España
🚌 1, 2, 44, 46, 74, 133,
202, circular
💰 Inexpensive. Free Sun
and Wed
♿ Few

Museo de América

TOP 25

An equestrian statue set in the form of a tree trunk (right) at the American Museum (left)

HIGHLIGHTS

● Sculptures of people with physical defects (Area 3)
● Canoe and tepee (Area 3)
● Statues of tribal chieftains (Area 3)
● Painting of *Entrance of Viceroy Morcillo into Potosí* (Area 3)
● Shrunken heads (Area 4)
● Mummy of Parácas (Area 4)
● Treasure of the Quimbayas (Area 4)
● 'Day of the Dead' paraphernalia (Area 4)
● Trocortesiano Maya Codex (Area 5)

This attractive museum can be seen either as an attempt to promote international understanding or as propaganda for the Spanish Conquest. Still, it makes a unique contribution to Spanish culture.

History Devoted to the presentation and explication of Pre-Columbian and Hispanic artefacts from Latin America, the America Museum, on the edge of the sprawling University area, is the best place in Spain to absorb the flavour of the culture of a different continent. Gold drew the Spanish to South America and gold draws visitors to marvel at the skills of the pre-Colombian artists. Many art works were melted down, so what is on show is even more important. Indeed, many South Americans living and working in Madrid are among the visitors. On Thursdays, the restaurant even serves an array of tasty South American dishes, such as *frijoles*, soups, Cuban-style rice and beans, green beans with tomatoes and spicy spaghetti.

Layout It's best to follow the suggested route, as it is easy to get confused. The collection is spread over two floors and five areas with different themes: the tools of understanding, the reality of America's society, religion and communication. Two particular highlights are the Treasure of the Quimbayas (Area 4), including exquisite gold figures, skull-cap helmets, drinking flasks, and trumpets from Colombia, and the Trocortesiano Maya Codex (Area 5), which records the arrival of the Spaniards in the New World and the Spanish Conquest in minute, intricate runes.

One of the men's costumes on display (right) at the Museum of Costume (left)

Museo del Traje

THE BASICS

www.meseodeltraje.mcu.es

🔵 C3

✉ Avenida Juan de Herrera 2

☎ 91 550 47 00

🕐 Tue–Sat 9.30–7, Sun and public hols 10–3

🍴 Café, restaurant

Ⓜ Moncloa, Ciudad Universitaria

🚌 46, 62, 82, 83, 132, 133

👟 Inexpensive. Free under 18, over 65, Sat after 2.30, Sun

♿ Good

Since its opening in 2004, the Museum of Costume has made its mark on the Madrid cultural stage. Far more than just clothes, the collection is a reflection of how Spanish society has changed over the centuries.

The collection In the 14 galleries of this elegant museum, the clothes are shown at different angles, so that you can see the front of some, the back of others. Through the glass, you can peer at centuries-old frock coats and silk doublets, and admire the embroidery on bodices. What you see is just a part of the collection that totals over 21,000 items. The galleries are organized chronologically, so that you can see how fashion and practicality evolved over centuries.

Hi-tech display Although historians are fascinated by the 13th-century trousseau of the daughter of Ferdinand III, most visitors are intrigued by a hi-tech display devoted to women's underwear. Virtual reality video twirls viewers from the bodices of the 17th century to the girdles of the 1940s. But there is everything in the museum, from Spanish *mantillas* to the latest shoes.

Of course, with rooms all to themselves are Spain's legendary fashion designers, such as Mariano Fortuny (born in Granada) and Cristóbal Balenciaga, a Basque who went on to take the Parisian fashion world by storm. Best of all, you can try on old-fashioned clothes to get a feel of how comfortable—or uncomfortable—they were.

HIGHLIGHTS

● The funerary apparel of Doña María, daughter of Fernando III
● 1740s silver frock coat
● Women's underwear
● Spanish headdresses
● Regional costume
● The genius of Fortuny
● Christian Dior clothes
● Pedro Rodríguez and the New Look
● The catwalk

TIPS

● Book up for a special meal at Bokado (▷ 41), the museum's own very posh restaurant. In summer, dine out on the terrace.
● Excellent shop, with high-quality silk ties, Spanish shawls and jewellery.

Palacio Real

HIGHLIGHTS

- Grand staircase
- Sala de Porcelana
- Salón de Alabarderos
- Salón de Columnas
- Sala de Gasparini
- Salón de Carlos III
- Clock collection
- Chapel by Giambattista Sacchetti and Ventura Rodríguez
- Music Museum
- Sabatini Gardens

TIP

- The Changing of the Guard takes place at noon on the first Wed of the month (except Jul, Aug, Sep).

The scale of the palace is awesome and the pomp overwhelming. The story that sentries guarding the rear of the building used to freeze to death in the icy wind adds to the sense of chilliness it inspires.

Scaled to fit The Royal Palace was begun under Philip V in 1737, after the old Muslim fortress was destroyed by fire in 1734. The original design by Filippo Juvanna was for façades measuring 475m (520 yards) each, or three times longer than the palace now, but there was neither the space nor the money for that. It was completed in 1764, to designs by Sacchetti. From the street side, it is a normal palatial building of the period, with Doric pilasters framing the reception hall windows. The royal family does not actually live here: it is used occasionally for state visits, during which dinner is

The façade of the Palacio Real (left); statues lining the approach (middle); guards outside the palace (right); changing of the guard (bottom left); the exterior of the Royal Palace (bottom middle); a guard taking part in the changing of the guard ceremony (bottom right)

served in the gala dining room. The entrance is to the south side of the building, across the Plaza de la Armería, which is flanked by the Royal Armoury housing El Cid's sword and the ornate armour of Carlos V and Felipe III.

Interior and gardens There are more than 3,000 rooms, and most are never used. A ceiling by Conrado Giaquinto accents the grand staircase. The ceiling of the Sala de Gasparini is remarkable, done in stucco, while the ceiling of the Sala de Porcelana, built for Charles III, has a fine display of white, gold and green porcelain plaques. To the north of the palace are the elegant Sabatini Gardens, which offer the best view of the palace, while to the rear is the Campo del Moro. The only way to see the palace is by following a fixed itinerary, which takes in the most impressive rooms.

THE BASICS

www.patrimonionacional.es

🔡 E7

✉ Calle Bailén

☎ 91 454 88 00

🕐 Apr–Sep Mon–Sat 9–6, Sun and public hols 9–3; Oct–Mar Mon–Sat 9.30–5, Sun and public hols 9–2

🚇 Ópera

🚌 3, 25, 33, 148

💷 Expensive. Free: children under 5, EU citizens on Wed

♿ Very good

Parque del Oeste

TOP 25

The rose garden (left); remains of the Templo de Debod (right)

THE BASICS

➕ C4
✉ Jardines del Paseo del Pintor Rosales
☎ 91 541 74 50
🕐 *Teleférico*: Sat, Sun and public hols 12–7
Ⓜ Argüelles
🚌 74, 84, 93

Templo de Debod

www.esmadrid.com
✉ Calle de Ferraz 1, Parque de la Montaña
☎ 91 366 74 15
🕐 Apr–Sep Tue–Fri 10–2, 6–8, Sat, Sun 10–2; Oct–Mar Tue–Fri 9.45–1.45, 4.15–6.15, Sat, Sun 10–2. Closed Mon and public hols
Ⓜ Plaza de España, Ventura Rodríguez
🚌 25, 33, 39, 46, 74, 75, 148
🎫 Free

HIGHLIGHTS

- *Teleférico*
- La Rosaleda
- Fuente (fountain)
- Statue of Juan de Villanueva
- Statue of Sor Juana Inés de la Cruz
- Statue of Simón Bolívar
- View over Casa de Campo
- Trees, including atlas cedar, cypress and magnolia

Less frequented and more informal than the Retiro, the Parque del Oeste is the best place in the city for a peaceful stroll in summer, particularly at the quieter northern end. Best avoided at night.

Rubbish dump to park Designed in the first years of the 20th century by landscape gardener Cecilio Rodríguez on what had previously been an immense rubbish heap, the Parque del Oeste was practically destroyed during the Civil War, when it provided a cover for the Republicans as the Nationalist troops invaded Madrid. Now rebuilt, it is still one of the city's most appealing and romantic open spaces. The park contains birch, fir, atlas cedar and cypress trees, among others, as well as a 17,000sq m (183,000sq ft) rose garden, La Rosaleda, which hosts a rose festival each May. The *teleférico* (cable car) in the park runs out to the Casa de Campo, affording bird's-eye views over the west of Madrid. In summer, elegant, noisy terrace bars are set up along the Paseo de Pintor Rosales, Ernest Hemingway's favourite street.

Templo de Debod It is somehow typical of Madrid that one of its most interesting attractions should not be Spanish at all. The Debod Temple, at the park's southern corner near Plaza de España, is a 4th-century BC Egyptian temple honouring the god Amon. It was installed in 1970 as a gift from the Egyptian government to Spanish engineers and archaeologists who had saved many treasures before large areas of land were flooded after the completion of the Aswan Dam.

Have an *aperitivo* on the terrace of the Café de Oriente, with the harmonious formal gardens stretching away in front of you to the Royal Palace. This is the place to reflect on the might of the monarchy at the height of its powers.

Ambitious emperor The elegant Plaza de Oriente was planned in 1811 under Joseph Bonaparte. To build it, he had to destroy the monuments and churches that then surrounded the Royal Palace. His original aim had been to build a kind of Champs-Élysées, running from the Plaza to the Cibeles Fountain. Fortunately, the Champs-Élysées project was abandoned; had it not been, Madrid would have lost, among many other treasures, the Monasterio de las Descalzas Reales (▷ 50; Convent of the Royal Shoeless Nuns). The existing square dates from the reign of Queen Isabella II (1833–1904). The attractively laid-out gardens contain statues of the kings and queens of Spain, which were originally intended for the top of the Royal Palace facing on to the plaza, but were never put into place because they were too heavy, and Isabella II dreamed that an earthquake made them topple over onto her.

Teatro Real At the eastern end of the square stands the Royal Theatre, built between 1818 and 1850 and now restored. The open-air building that originally occupied the site was expanded in 1737 for a visit by Farinelli, the legendary *castrato* singer, of whom Philip V (1683–1746) was particularly fond.

THE BASICS

🞧 E7
🗺 Plaza de Oriente
🍴 Café de Oriente
🚇 Ópera
🚌 3, 25, 33

HIGHLIGHT

● The equestrian statue in the middle of the square of Philip IV by Montañes, taken from a portrait by Velàzquez

PALACIO AND THE WEST

★ **TOP 25**

More to See

BASILICA DE SAN FRANCISCO EL GRANDE

Built between 1761 and 1784, this church has a neoclassical façade by Francisco Sabatini, one of the greatest practitioners of this style, and an overwhelming 33m (108ft) dome by Miguel Fernández. The monastery was used as a barracks from 1835, after which it was lavishly redecorated. The interior (note the ceiling frescoes) contains much work by Spanish masters, including an early Goya, *The Sermon of San Bernadino de Siena*, in the first chapel on the left. There is also a museum.

➕ E8 ✉ Plaza de San Francisco, Calle de San Buenaventura 1 ☎ 91 365 38 00 🕐 Sep–Jul Tue–Fri 11–12.30, 4–6.30, Sat 11–1.30; Aug Tue–Sun 11–12.30, 5–7.30 🚇 La Latina 🚌 3, 17, 18, 23, 35, 41, 60, 138 ♿ None

ESTACIÓN DE PRÍNCIPE PÍO

www.renfe.es

Restored and modernized, what was once the important Estación del Norte (North Station) is now both a busy commuter railway station for the suburbs and a lively destination shopping complex (▶ 39), with cinemas in the Centro de Ocio (leisure centre). There is also an important bus station outside what is still a handsome building, dating from the late 19th century. The station takes its name from Príncipe Pío, the nearby hill, where Spanish rebels were shot by French soldiers on 3 May 1808.

➕ D6 ✉ Paseo de la Florida, corner of Cuesta de San Vicente 🚇 Metro Príncipe Pío 🚌 25, 33, 39, 41, 46, 75, 138

JARDINES DE LAS VISTILLAS

The best place in Madrid for sunset-watching, this park has wonderful views over the Casa de Campo towards the Guadarrama Mountains. From late spring to autumn it's also a lively place to go for an evening drink.

➕ D8 ✉ Travesia Vistillas 🚇 Ópera, La Latina 🚌 3, 148

MURALLA ARABE

What little we can see of the Arab Wall is the oldest surviving part of Madrid. It

A café on Plaza de España

was originally part of the walls of the small Arab town of Magerit. The area around it, now the Parque Emir Mohammed I, is one of the venues for the autumn arts festival.

➕ D8 ✉ Cuesta de la Vega 🚇 Ópera
🚌 3, 41, 148

PLAZA DE ESPAÑA

A statue of Cervantes stands at the western end of this grandiose square, overlooking a rather lovable 1815 statue of his two legendary creations, Don Quixote and Sancho Panza. On the edge of the square, with a neo-baroque doorway, is the Edificio España, Madrid's first true skyscraper, while the 137m (450ft) Torre Madrid was a symbol of post-Civil War economic recovery and Europe's tallest building when it was built in 1957.

➕ E6 ✉ Plaza de España 🚇 Plaza de España 🚌 68, 69, 74, 133

SAN NICOLÁS DE LOS SERVITAS

This is Madrid's oldest church and though much restored after the Civil War, its tower is one of the very few echoes of the Arabic Madrid in the city. Designated a National Monument, the tower is probably the minaret of a mosque later consecrated as a Catholic church. This 12th-century tower is Mudéjar (built by Muslims under Christian rule), while the central apse is Gothic. Juan de Herrera, employed by Philip II as the architect of El Escorial, was buried in the crypt in 1597.

➕ E7 ✉ Plaza de San Nicolás 6 ☎ 91 548 83 14 🕐 Mon 8.30–2, Sun 10–2, 6.30–8.30; do not visit during Mass. Not always open; advance phone call advisable 🚇 Ópera, Sol ♿ None

VIADUCTO

Viaducto was known as 'the Suicide Bridge' until the city council put up suicide-proof screens in 1997. Unfortunately these detract from the drama of the views down on the Calle de Segovia far below.

➕ E8 ✉ Calle Bailén 🚇 Ópera 🚌 3, 148

Plaza de España

A Walk West from Sol

Stroll through some of Madrid's oldest streets and squares; take in the grandeur of the Palace and gardens.

DISTANCE: 5km (3 miles)   **ALLOW:** 2–3 hours

START

PUERTA DEL SOL
➕ F7 🚇 Puerta del Sol

END

ARGÜELLES
➕ D5 🚇 Argüelles

1 Leave the Puerta del Sol at the western end and take Calle de Postas up to Plaza Mayor. Cross the plaza and exit at the diagonally opposite corner (El Arco de los Cuchilleros).

2 At the bottom of the steps cross the street and go down Calle del Maestro de la Villa and into the Plaza Conde de Barajas.

3 Cross the square, turn right on Calle del Conde Miranda, right again on Calle del Codo and into the Plaza de la Villa.

4 Cross Calle Mayor and follow Calle de los Señores de Luzon to the Plaza de Ramales. Cross the square and go downhill to Calle de Lepanto, which leads to the Plaza de Oriente.

7 Follow the path around to the right and continue up to the *Teleférico*. Take a ride for fantastic views or cross Paseo Pintor Rasales and walk up Calle de Marqués Urquijo to Argüelles Metro station.

6 Bear left, following the broad pavement to steps leading up the mound to the Templo de Debod. Walk past the temple to admire the views, descend the steps and turn right for the bandstand. Look down the hill to the Rosaleda rose garden.

5 Turn left and walk past the statues to the Palacio Real. Turn right and follow the promenade, walking along the Sabatini Gardens. Do not go down into the tunnel, but climb the steps on the left and continue across the bottom of the Plaza de España.

Shopping

BERBERÍA DEL SAHARA Y EL SAHEL

The name of this shop is a clue: come here for unusual and authentic materials and crafts from North Africa and the Sahara region. What makes it different is space devoted to exhibitions, travel guides and other information on the region.

🔲 E8 ✉ Redondilla 8 ☎ 91 354 01 76 🚇 La Latina

CENTRO COMERCIAL PRÍNCIPE PÍO

www.ccprincipepio.com
This conversion of a railway station (the 1881 Estacíon del Norte) is a fine example of the imaginative recycling of old buildings that is going on in Madrid. Not far from the Royal Palace and the Catedral de la Almudena, find fashion in the basement and, restaurants on the ground floor, as well as cinemas.

🔲 D6 ✉ Paseo de la Florida ☎ 91 758 00 40 🚇 Príncipe Pío

Some outstanding Spanish stores in this shopping complex include:

LURUEÑA

www.luruena.es
Leather in all shapes and sizes, from practical shoes and bags, to sandals and high heels. Men can find a full range, from formal office wear to casual vacation shoes; women have an even wider choice, with jazzy party bags and purses.
☎ 91 542 04 79

MASSIMO DUTTI WOMAN

www.massimodutti.com
This is an international Spanish company, despite its Italian name. Known for its classy style at mid-range prices, this store is devoted to women's clothing, as well as fragrances.
☎ 91 541 08 07

PULL & BEAR

www.pullbear.com
Appealing to the young market, this is another great Spanish fashion industry success story. Great fun, good prices.
☎ 91 542 06 91

SHOES

Thanks to its centuries-old leather industry, Spain has long had a love affair with *zapatos* (shoes). Many of the world's leading designers are Spanish, mainly from Alicante, Valencia and the Balearic Islands. They range from the extremely expensive (Loewe) to the extremely popular (Camper). And the choice for men's and children's shoes is almost as wide as for women's. Known for its outlet shops with bargain prices is Calle de Augusto Figueroa in Chueca.

TINO GONZÁLEZ

www.tinogonzalez.com
For imaginative yet practical shoes for men, women and children, Tino González has a wide range on offer from formal to informal—and that special party pair.
☎ 91 632 44 90

TRUCCO

Rather than fashionistas, Trucco appeals to women with flair, who value attention to detail and quality. This is another popular and reliable Spanish-made international fashion franchise.
☎ 91 542 74 36

***

MUSEO DEL TRAJE

This museum (▷ 31) has one of the best gift shops around, with special emphasis on clothing, from Spanish *mantillas* to elegant silk ties, plus wonderful jewellery.

🔲 C3 ✉ 2 Avenida Juan de Herrera ☎ 91 550 47 00 🚇 Moncloa, Ciudad Universitaria

TONI MARTIN

www.tonimartindiscos.com
This music shop, specializing in country, jazz and rock 'n' roll, stocks a great selection of CDs and vinyl, new and second-hand.

🔲 E6 ✉ Calle Martin de los Heros 18 ☎ 91 542 50 20 🚇 Plaza de España

Entertainment and Nightlife

ALPHAVILLE

Alphaville opened shortly after democracy came to Spain. It shows international films in original versions with Spanish subtitles. Late-night showings on weekends and a good café downstairs.

🔹 E6 ✉ Calle Martín de los Heros 14 ☎ 91 547 4357 🎵 Plaza de España

BALCÓN DE ROSALES

www.balconderosales.com
Near the university district, this striking modern nightclub has three areas. As well as a well-priced restaurant and lounge section, there is the Café Teatro, a large dance floor with great views over the Parque del Oeste. Open from 11pm till 5am, entry is free, but drinks are expensive.

🔹 D5 ✉ Paseo Pintor Rosales at Marqués de Urquijo ☎ 618 69 64 38 🎵 Argüelles

CHESTERFIELD CAFÉ

Bands from Europe and the US perform rock and blues live Wed–Sat in this American-style café-bar, which serves hamburgers and french fries, ribs and pasta dishes. There is a good choice of beers and cocktails.

🔹 D/E5 ✉ Calle Serrano Jovér 5 ☎ 91 542 28 17 🎵 Argüelles

COPÉRNICO NOVA CLUB

Close to the university campus, this is the place

to hear live bands from every part of the spectrum, from punk to metal. The décor is themed on a galleon, with telescopes and globes. Reasonable door charges, open 11pm–6am.

🔹 E4 ✉ Calle Fernández de los Ríos 67 ☎ 91 559 59 22 🎵 Moncloa

ELANUET

For anyone young or old, who reckons that music was better in the '80s, this is the place for techno pop.

🔹 E8 ✉ Calle Segovia 24 ☎ No phone 🎵 Wed–Sun 10pm–3.30am 🎵 La Latina

EL LIMBO

With clips from films projected onto screens, live bands and DJs, this is a popular venue with teenagers on a night out.

BOOM INDUSTRY

There are at least 60 cinemas in Madrid. Most have a discount day (Monday or Wednesday), when tickets are half price. Always arrive well in advance for evening weekend showings; queues can start forming an hour before projection time. Bigger cinemas now have advanced reservations and most have reserved seating on weekends. Movie information is published in full in all the daily newspapers: earliest showings (*pasos*) are generally at 4, latest at 10.30.

🔹 E8 ✉ Calle Bailén 39 ☎ 91 365 21 58 🎵 Mon–Sat 10pm–3.30am 🎵 La Latina

MARULA CAFÉ

www.marulacafe.com
Soulfood sessions, funk and more at this popular club with live DJs. Cool bar, outdoor terrace in summer.

🔹 E8 ✉ Calle Caños Viejos 3 ☎ 91 366 15 96 🎵 Nightly 11pm–6am 🎵 La Latina

PRINCESA

Since it opened in the mid 1990s, this has become the city's main screening point for new Spanish films.

🔹 E6 ✉ Calle Princesa 3 ☎ 91 541 41 00 🎵 Plaza de España

RENOIR

The best of the cinemas clustered around the bottom of Calle Martín de los Heros, near the Plaza de España, shows the latest art films. Detailed information sheets are published (in Spanish) to accompany each one. There are late showings on weekends.

🔹 E6 ✉ Calle Martín de los Heros 12 ☎ 91 541 41 00 🎵 Plaza de España

TEATRO REAL

www.teatro-real.com
The grandest and most beautiful of the European opera houses.

🔹 E7 ✉ Plaza de Isabel II ☎ 91 516 06 60/902 24 48 48 🎵 Ópera

Restaurants

PRICES

Prices are approximate, based on a 3-course meal for one person.

€€€ over €45
€€   €25–€45
€   under €25

A'CASIÑA (€€)

The Columnas, just one of the restaurant's large dining areas, is a sunlit indoor terrace overlooking the park. Start with *arroz caldoso con bogavante*, a rich lobster soup cooked with rice and follow up with the hake (*merluza*). Reservations essential.
🚇 B7/8 ✉ Avenida de Angel, Casa de Campo ☎ 91 526 34 25 🕐 Closed Sun night 🚇 Lago

BOKADO (€€€)

With its cool modern interior and summer terrace, the Santamaría brothers' high-class Basque restaurant must be one of the world's best places to eat in a museum. In the Museo del Traje (▷ 31), book up for Basque seafood treats, where dishes are as eye-catching and creative as the clothes.
🚇 C3 ✉ Avenida de Juan de Herrera 2 ☎ 91 549 00 41 🕐 Closed Sun, Mon 🚇 Ciudad Universitaria, Moncloa

LA BOLA TABERNA (€€)

www.labola.es
La Bola is really an old tavern, boasting a century in business. It's best known for its *cocido madrileño* (a soup-style stew with noodles, chickpeas, meat and vegetables), presented in a sizzling pot. No credit cards.
🚇 E7 ✉ Calle de la Bola 5 ☎ 91 547 69 30 🕐 Closed Sun night 🚇 Ópera, Santo Domingo

CAFÉ DE ORIENTE (€€)

Built on the remains of a convent and facing the Royal Palace, this is a rather aristocratic place with distinctive dishes that fuse *madrileño* with French cuisine.

REGIONAL CUISINE

Spanish regional cuisine—particularly that of the Basque country—has achieved greater international recognition than the cuisine of Madrid itself. Basque and Catalan cuisine tends to be fish-based, though if you do order meat, it is likely to come in the form of a huge steak. Basque tapas are available at some of the Basque restaurants; these are little culinary works of art. Galician specialties include seafood and hearty peasant dishes. The Asturians are known for their cider and *fabadas*, bean-based stews.

🚇 E7 ✉ Plaza de Oriente 2 ☎ 91 547 15 64/91 541 39 74 🚇 Ópera

CASA MINGO (€)

A popular Asturian *sidrería* or cider house. The idea is to pour the cider into the glass from a great height and drink it very fast. The best tapas are based on the strong Cabrales cheese. The restaurant is excellent.
🚇 C6 ✉ Paseo de la Florida 34 ☎ 91 547 79 18 🚇 Príncipe Pío

DANTXARI (€€–€€€)

This Basque tavern has spicy cod, lamb with garlic and wild mushrooms. Wide-ranging Spanish wine list and cheerful service.
🚇 F6 ✉ Ventura Rodriguez 8 ☎ 91 542 35 24 🕐 Lunch, dinner. Closed Sun, public hols 🚇 Ventura Rodríguez

EL INGENIO (€€)

This restaurant, close to Plaza Santo Domingo, serves traditional Spanish cuisine. You'll find salads, croquettes, wild mushrooms with aioli, vegetable stew, dried butterbean dishes and fresh cod on the menu. The place has a literary feel—Don Quixote paraphernalia adorn the walls. Reserving in advance is advisable, as it's a popular place.
🚇 E6 ✉ Calle de Leganitos 10 ☎ 91 541 91 33 🕐 Closed Sun, public hols 🚇 Santo Domingo

MESÓN CINCO JOTAS (€€)

One of a chain of well-run Cinco Jotas (5 Js) that pride themselves on serving the best quality (5 star, or 5 J) Iberian ham from Jabugo. Choose between the restaurant and the tapas bar.
🔀 E3 ✉ Paseo de San Francisco de Sales 27 ☎ 91 544 01 89 🕙 Daily 12.30–midnight, weekends till 1am 🚇 Islas Filipinas

MI PUEBLO (€€)

www.restaurantemipueblo.es
This small restaurant has a loyal clientele attracted by the cosy ambience and traditional home cooking (cocina casera). It is one of only a few places serving a local wine—from Arganda del Rey, south of the city.
🔀 E7 ✉ Costanilla de Santiago 2 ☎ 91 548 20 73 🕙 Closed Sun night, Mon 🚇 Ópera

EL MOLINO DE LOS PORCHES (€€€)

Join throngs of locals who come for asado, the roast meat that is both the house speciality and a Castilian speciality. Old-fashioned and proud of it. Popular summer garden dining. Important to book.
🔀 D5 ✉ Paseo Pintor Rosales 1 ☎ 91 548 13 36 🕙 Daily noon–midnight 🚇 Argüelles

PRADA A TOPE (€€)

Rustic and comfortable, this tavern is enhanced with aged-wood fittings. The cuisine is from León, which is known for its smoked beef, and this restaurant does it proud. Cocido, tortilla, roast beef and spicy green peppers are all on the menu. One of a group, with two branches in Madrid.
🔀 D7 ✉ Cuesta de San Vicente 32 ☎ 91 559 39 53 🕙 Closed Tue 🚇 Plaza de España, Príncipe Pío
Also: 🔀 G7 ✉ Príncipe 11 ☎ 91 429 59 21 🕙 Closed Sun dinner, Mon 🚇 Sevilla

SAL GORDA (€€)

This long-established restaurant is off the beaten tourist trail and popular with locals for its dishes: Spanish through and through. Excellent value for money.
🔀 E2 ✉ Beatriz de Bobadilla 9 ☎ 91 553 95 06 🕙 Closed Sun, Aug 🚇 Guzmán el Bueno

---

REGIONAL FARE

After the Basques, the Galicians have the best cuisine in Spain. Together with their neighbours the Asturians, they prefer maritime cuisine, and the portions are generally sizeable, with potatoes the staple food. Regional special dishes include pulpo (octopus), and pimentos de Padrón (hot green peppers)—best eaten with a jug of water.

SANLÚCAR (€)

www.barsanlucar.tk
A classic Andalucian-style tapas bar with owners from Cadiz, so sherries are the perfect accompaniment for prawns, langostinos (crayfish) and other seafood. Well-priced three-course menu of the day.
🔀 E8 ✉ San Isidro Labrador 14 ☎ 91 354 00 52 🕙 Closed Sun dinner, Mon 🚇 La Latina

EL SENADOR (€€)

This well-established traditional restaurant serves Segovian cuisine. The house special is roast lamb, but there are also steaks cooked on a charcoal fire and fresh fish. The wine is great, and so are the desserts. Tapas are available at the bar. Reserve in advance.
🔀 E7 ✉ Plaza de la Marina Española 2 ☎ 91 541 22 21 🕙 Closed Sun night 🚇 Santo Domingo, Ópera

LA TAQUERÍA DE BIRRA (€)

www.lastaquerias.com
Where locals come to get their fill of Mexican dishes, such as tacos (including vegetarian tacos). Jolly atmosphere with Mexican music.
🔀 E8 ✉ Don Pedro 11 ☎ 91 366 45 39 🕙 Daily 7.30–2.30am; weekends, public hols 1pm–2.30am 🚇 Ópera

This is the Madrid that most visitors expect to see: medieval lanes, great art museums, tapas bars on every corner. It's best explored on foot.

CALLE DE FUENCARRAL

Calle de las Infantas

Calle de la Reina

GRAN VIA

San José

Calle de Jardines

Sevilla

Montera

SOL

Calatravas

Calle de la Aduana

ALCALÁ

Real Academia
DE de Bellas Artes

Banco de
España

CALLE

Teatro
Alcázar

Calle de los Madrazo

CARRERA

Calle de Zorilla

Museo
Thyssen-
Bornemisza

DE SAN JERÓNIMO

PASEO DEL PRADO

CORTES

Plaza de
las Cortes

Plaza de
Santa Ana

Ateneo

Plaza
Cánovas
del Castillo

Calle de la Cruz

Calle de Echegaray

Calle del Prado

Plaza del
Angel

Casa Museo
Lope de Vega

Calle de Cervantes

Jesús de
Medinaceli

San
Sebastián

Calle
de Atocha

Plaza
Matute

Calle
de las
Trinitarias

Plaza
Jesús

Calle Lope de Vega

Calle Huertas

Calle Santa María

Plaza de
Antón
Martín

Plaza
Platería
Martínez

de Magdalena

Calle de Moratín

San
Roberto

Calle de Fúcar

Calle de la Cabeza

Calle del Olmo

Calle de la Alameda

Calle del Gobernador

Anton Martin

Calle Almadén

Calle de la Cabeza

Calle del Olivar

Calle de Avemaría

Calle Torrecilla del Leal

Calle

Turrie

de

Atocha

PASEO DEL PRADO

Lavapiés

Calle la Fe

Calle de Salitre

Santa

Isabel

Conservatorio
de Música

Plaza
Lavapiés

Calle Dr Piga

Convento de
Santa Isabel

Atocha

Plaza del
Emperador
Carlos V

Calle San
Lorenzo

de

Museo Nacional
Reina Sofía

PASEO DE SANTA MARÍA DE LA CABEZA

Calle Tribulete

Calle Miguel Servet

Calle Valencia

Calle Amparo

Argumosa

ATOCHA

RONDA DE VALENCIA

RONDA

DE

María
Auxiliadora

Circo

Embajadores

G

H

The museum's glass elevators (opposite, left and right); Picasso's Guernica (middle)

Museo Nacional Reina Sofía

In Madrid's leading modern art museum, the home of Picasso's _Guernica_, you might not like all the works on display. But even on its busiest days, the light and airy space is a delight.

A triumph of planning Inspired by the Pompidou Centre in Paris, this 12,540sq m (135,000sq ft) space is Madrid's finest contemporary art museum; among European museums only the Pompidou is larger. It occupies a building that served as the San Carlos hospital between 1977 and 1986. Transparent elevators on the outside whisk you up for a thrilling view over the rooftops of Madrid. The fine permanent collection showcases Spanish art of the 20th century—cubism, surrealism, realism, informalism. The dramatic extension by French architect Jean Nouvel opened in 2004. Under the red roof are galleries for temporary exhibitions, as well as the library, shop, café and auditorium.

Guernica Picasso's masterpiece dominates the Reina Sofía. When it was commissioned by the Republican Government for display at the 1937 Paris Exhibition, the only instruction was that it be big: it measures 6.4 x 7m (21 x 23ft). Taking his inspiration from the Nationalist bombing of the Basque town of Guernica in 1937, this painting has become 20th-century art's great anti-war symbol. Many saw the 1995 decision to remove the bullet-proof screen that had protected it for many years as a symbolic gesture, showing that democracy in Spain had finally taken root.

THE BASICS

www.museoreinasofia.es
🚼 G9
✉ Calle Santa Isabel 52
☎ 91 467/ 50 62
🕐 Mon, Wed–Sat 10–9, Sun 10–2.30
🍴 Bar, restaurant
Ⓜ Atocha
🚌 6, 10, 14, 24, 26, 27, 32, 34, 36, 37, 41, 45, 47, 54, 56, 57, 85, 86
🚆 Atocha
💷 Moderate. Free under 18, over 65; Sat afternoon and Sun
♿ Very good

HIGHLIGHTS

- View from exterior elevators
- Enclosed patio
- _Guernica_, Picasso
- Joan Gris Room
- Picasso Room
- Joan Miró Room
- Dalí Room
- Surrealism Room
- Luis Buñuel Room
- Spanish 20th-Century Art Room

Museo Thyssen-Bornemisza

HIGHLIGHTS

● *Portrait of Giovanna Tornabuoni*, Domenico Ghirlandaio
● *Portrait of Henry VIII*, Holbein
● *St. Catherine of Alexandria*, Caravaggio
● *Annunciation Diptych*, Van Eyck
● *St. Jerome in the Wilderness*, Titian
● *The Lock*, Constable
● *Easter Morning*, Caspar David Friedrich
● *Les Vessenots*, Van Gogh
● *Man with a Clarinet*, Picasso

TIP

● In summer, the rooftop terrace is open for romantic dinners. Also in summer, the museum is open on Monday, and late at night.

This is one of the best things that has happened to Madrid since the end of the Civil War. It is also one of the few internationally renowned art museums where everything is priority viewing.

New museum The collection was begun by the German financier and industrialist Baron Heinrich Thyssen-Bornemisza in the 1920s and continued after his death by his son, Hans Heinrich (who died in 2002). The 775 paintings exhibited here were sold to the Spanish state for a mere $350 million in 1993, one year after the museum opened to the public. The permanent collection, spanning seven centuries, is housed in the sympathetically renovated 18th-century Palacio de Villahermosa. In 2004, the glass pavilion opened. It contains 19th- and 20th-century paintings from the collection of Hans Heinrich's widow, Carmen Thyssen-Bornemisza, a former Miss Spain.

The collection The sheer variety of the many works on display prompted some to call the Thyssen over-eclectic; others claim its very quirkiness is part of its charm. Each room highlights a different period: the top floor is devoted to art from medieval times through to the 17th century; the second floor to rococo and neoclassicism of the 18th and 19th centuries through to fauvism and expressionism; the first level to 20th-century surrealism, pop art and the avant-garde. Start from the top and work your way down. It is worth renting an audio guide, available in Spanish, English, French, German and Italian. The museum's shop is one of the best, whether you are looking for art books or beautiful gifts.

THE BASICS

www.museothyssen.org
🚹 G7
✉ Paseo del Prado 8
☎ 91 369 01 51
🕐 Tue–Sun 10–7
🍴 Café, restaurant
Ⓜ Banco de España
🚌 1, 2, 5, 9, 10, 14, 15, 20, 27, 34, 37, 45, 51, 52, 53, 74, 146, 150
🚉 Atocha, Recoletos
♿ Moderate. Free children under 12, reduction over 65
❓ Bookstore on the ground floor
♿ Excellent

Monasterio de las Descalzas Reales

TOP 25

Marble tomb of the Empress Maria (left) at the Monasterio de las Descalzas Reales (right)

THE BASICS

www.patrimonionacional.es
+ F7
✉ Plaza de las Descalzas Reales 3
☎ 91 454 88 00
🕐 Tue, Wed, Thu, Sat 10.30–12.30, 4–5, Fri 10.30–12.30, Sun and public hols 11–1.30
🚇 Sol, Ópera
🚌 3, 5, 150
♿ None
💶 Moderate. Free Wed to EU citizens

HIGHLIGHTS

● *Recumbent Christ,* Gaspar Becerra
● *Neapolitan Nativity* (Chapel of St. Michael)
● *Bust of the Mater Dolorosa,* José Risueño
● *Cardinal Infante Don Fernando of Austria,* Rubens
● *The Ship of the Church,* 16th-century painting
● *Adoration of the Magi,* Brueghel
● *The Empress María,* Goya
● *17th-century tapestries*

Though the tour of the Royal Shoeless Nuns' Convent is conducted at a brisk pace, the building contains an unusually high proportion of unmissable treasures.

Convent history Of Madrid's two monastery museums, the Descalzas Reales is the richer; most of its rooms are small museums in themselves. Founded by Juana of Austria, the younger daughter of Charles V, on the site of the place in which she was born, it was built between 1559 and 1564 in Madrid brick by Antonio Silla and Juan Bautista of Toledo. The whole place breathes mid-17th-century religious mysticism, though the 'vile stink' of which traveller William Beckford complained when attending Mass in the late 18th century has departed. The original sisters were all of noble or aristocratic blood, and each founded a chapel on reception into the order: there are 33 of them, and to this day the convent is home to 23 Franciscan nuns, each of whom maintains one of the chapels. The Grand Staircase, with its *trompe l'oeil* portrait of Philip IV and his family standing on the balcony, is covered with frescoes by the artist Claudio Coello. With its incongruous location right in the middle of commercial Madrid, it is a small miracle that it remains intact.

Seeing the collection The only way to see the convent is to take a tour. Given in Spanish only, it lasts around 45 minutes and is conducted at such a frenzied pace that it is worth buying a guide book at the entrance. The church can be visited only during Mass, at 8am or 7pm.

The cobbled Plaza Mayor strikes a chord with everyone entering it for the first time: it's here that you fully realize you are in the capital of Spain. Surely it is only in Madrid that a building as old as the Casa de la Panadería could have been frescoed over 400 years later.

Work in progress Built in the 15th century as a market square, and later renamed the Plaza del Arrabal (Square outside the Walls), the Plaza Mayor came into its own when Philip II, after making Madrid the capital of Spain, ordered it rebuilt as the administrative centre of the Court. The only part to be completed immediately was the Panadería, or the bakery, by architect Diego Sillero in 1590 (the frescoes are the work of the early 1990s), while the rest of it was completed in 1619 by Juan Gómez de la Mora under Philip III, whose bronze statue stands in the middle. After a fire in 1790, much of the square had to be rebuilt. The buildings between the towers on either side are Town Hall offices; the rest are private homes.

A gathering place The Plaza Mayor was where the more important members of the Court lived during the 17th century; at the end of the century, the square became the site of mounted bullfights, carnivals and the terrible *autos da fé* of the Spanish Inquisition, attended by thousands on 30 June 1680, when 118 offenders were executed in a single day. Hangings were also carried out here until the end of the 18th century. On a happier note, the plaza hosts the annual Christmas market.

THE BASICS

✚ F7/8
✉ Plaza Mayor
🍴 *Terraza* bars around square
Ⓜ Sol, Ópera
🚌 3, 5, 51, 52, 53, 150
❓ Tourist office in square

TIP

● In May, free concerts are held during the 2 May and San Isidro festivities

Puerta del Sol

The bear and tree, symbol of Madrid (left); statue of Carlos III (middle and right)

THE BASICS

☩ F7
✉ Puerta del Sol
🚇 Sol
🚌 3, 5, 15, 20, 51, 52, 150

HIGHLIGHTS

● Bear and *madroño* (strawberry tree) statue
● Statue of Charles III
● La Mallorquina pastry shop
● Newspaper stands: a major part of Madrid streetlife
● Tio Pepe sign
● Kilometre Zero
● Doña Manolita's lottery ticket kiosk

Almost inevitably, you will cross this square several times. For many *madrileños*, it is the true soul of the city and each year thousands gather here to see in the New Year.

Soul of Madrid The area's namesake gateway was demolished in 1570 when the square was widened to receive Anne of Austria, Philip II's fourth wife. The design of the present square dates back to 1861; the building on the south side, the Casa de Correos, is from 1768. Originally the Post Office, it is now the headquarters of the Madrid regional government. Spain's Kilometre Zero, the point from which all distances in Spain are measured, can be found on the pavement in front of it. The clock and tower were built in 1867.

A troubled past The Esquilache mutiny of 1766 began here, sparked by Charles III's uncharacteristically tyrannical insistence that the population should wear short capes and three-cornered hats to emulate a hated French style. The most notable moment in Sol's history was on 2 and 3 May 1808, when *madrileños* took up arms against occupying French troops, a heroic resistance in which more than 2,000 died, immortalized in Goya's two magnificent anti-war paintings in the Prado, *Dos de Mayo* and *Tres de Mayo*. It was here, also, that politician José Canalejas was assassinated in 1912, and the Second Republic was proclaimed in 1931. It remains a popular meeting place, especially by the monument of the bear with a strawberry tree, the symbol of Madrid.

TOP 25

El Rastro

THE BASICS

⊞ F9

✉ Ribera de Curtidores

🕑 9–3

🚇 Tirso de Molina

🍴 Many cafés and bars

HIGHLIGHTS

● Street vendors shouting
● Spanish pottery
● Antiques at Galerías Piquer
● Leather boots and saddles
at Curtidos Roman, Calle
Ribera de Curtidores 16

For locals and visitors alike, this is the classic place to spend a Sunday morning. The Rastro is much more than a flea market; crowds bustle as if they are off to a football match. Be careful with your valuables.

Bargains galore Start from the Tirso de Molina Metro station, and head for the Plaza de Cascorro. The lines of stalls run downhill, along both sides and in the middle of the Ribera de Curtidores street, and go on to form a busy triangle with Calle de Toledo and Calle Embajadores. It all gets under way at 9am, and the trick is to take your time and to tuck all your valuables away. Bargains are here for those who poke, prod and haggle for old birdcages and cheap underwear, leather bags and clay pots.

A bloody history But it is not just the main street. All the regular shops are open, and the market spills into the side streets. Find pets on Calle de Fray Ceferino González, and every sort of painting, from watercolours and prints to original oils, on the Calle de San Cayetano, nicknamed the Painters' Street. Drop by the Galerías Piquér (▷ 62), a courtyard surrounded by antiques shops. As for the name, *rastro* dates back to the 16th century, when this was the site of a slaughterhouse. When the dead animals were dragged away to the tanners (*curtidores*), they left a *rastro*, trail of blood on the street.

CENTRO ★ **TOP 25**

Real Academia de Bellas Artes

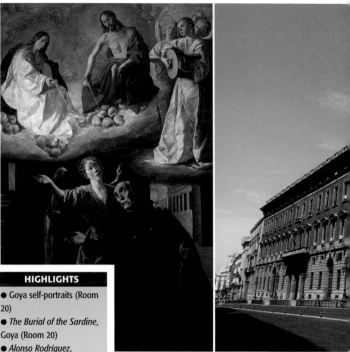

HIGHLIGHTS

● Goya self-portraits (Room 20)
● *The Burial of the Sardine*, Goya (Room 20)
● *Alonso Rodríguez*, Francisco Zurbarán (Room 6)
● *Head of John the Baptist*, José de Ribera (Room 3)
● *Felipe IV*, Velázquez (Room 11)
● *Susana and the Elders*, Rubens (Room 13)
● *Spring*, Giuseppe Arcimboldo (Room 14)
● Goya etchings (Calcografía Nacional)

TIP

● Don't miss the Calcografía Nacional, with its room dedicated to Goya's disturbing engravings.

The Prado, Thyssen and Reina Sofía may have more visitors, but the eclectic collections of the Royal Academy of Fine Arts, the oldest permanent art institution in Madrid, are interesting to visit.

History It was Francisco Meléndez who suggested the establishment of a Royal Academy on the model of those in Rome, Paris, Florence and other great cities. Work began on the authorization of Philip V in 1744 and was completed under Fernando VI in 1752. The Academy was initially in the Casa de la Panadería, in the Plaza Mayor, but Charles III transferred it to its present site in 1773. The original building was baroque, but shortly after it opened, Academy members with conservative tastes insisted that it be given today's neoclassical façade. Rarely overcrowded, it is small enough to be visited comfortably in a couple of hours.

Layout The museum has three floors. The best-known galleries are on the second floor, most notably Room 20, with its Goyas. Other highlights by 17th-century Spanish artists include *Head of John the Baptist* by José de Ribera (1591–1652), *Alonso Rodríguez* by Francisco Zurbarán, and *Felipé IV* by Velázquez. *Spring,* by the 16th-century Milanese painter Giuseppe Arcimboldo, in Room 14, is the only Arcimboldo in Spain and one of only a handful in the world. Halfway up the stairs to the entrance (and easily missed) is another museum, La Calcografía Nacional, or Engraving Plates Museum. The Gabinete Goya at the back of this contains a beautifully displayed series of the original plates used by the artist for his etchings.

THE BASICS

http://rabasf.insde.es
✚ G7
✉ Calle Alcalá 13
☎ 91 524 08 64
🕐 Tue–Fri 9–7, Sat–Mon and public hols 9–2.30
🚇 Sol, Sevilla
🚌 3, 5, 15, 20, 51, 52, 150
💶 Inexpensive. Free under 18, over 65; Wed
♿ Limited

More to See

ARCO DE LOS CUCHILLEROS

Connecting the Plaza Mayor to the Cava Baja, this 18th-century archway is a landmark for both residents and tourists, who often use it as an easy-to-find meeting place. All around are some of the most popular old bars and taverns in the city. Its name comes from the cutlers and knife makers who once worked here, making and honing knives for the nearby butchers, as well as swords for the nobility.

🕂 E8 ✉ Plaza Mayor ⊙ Sol, Ópera 🚌 3, 5, 51, 52, 53, 150

CALLE ARENAL

Connecting Sol with Ópera, the Calle Arenal has a 19th-century air. During the Middle Ages, it was no more than a ravine, but after 1656, it began to compete with the Calle Mayor in importance, perhaps because it was the shortest route between the Royal Palace and Sol.

🕂 F7 ⊙ Sol, Ópera 🚌 5, 15, 20, 51, 52, 53, 150

CALLE MAYOR

This is perhaps the most traditional of Madrid's streets, with some fusty, old-fashioned shops—including a wonderful *guitarrería* (guitar store) near the Calle Bailén end. Spain's two greatest playwrights, Lope de Vega and Calderón de la Barca, lived at Nos. 25 and 61 respectively.

🕂 E/F7 ⊙ Sol 🚌 3

CALLE DEL MESÓN DE PAREDES

To get a complete sense of the slightly surreal and multicultural atmosphere of Madrid's *barrio popular*, stroll down this street and those around it on any weekday morning when it is bustling and full of life. La Corrala is an 1882 example of the corridor-tenement found throughout working-class Madrid. Beginning in the early 1980s, it was used for productions as an open-air theatre. It is now an Artistic Monument.

🕂 F9 ⊙ Tirso de Molina, Lavapies 🚌 32, 57

Gran Vía

CASA MUSEO LOPE DE VEGA
www.rae.es

Spain's greatest playwright, Felix Lope de Vega (1562–1635), lived in this house from 1610 until his death. Now an evocative museum, the rooms are furnished in the style of the period, based on an inventory by Lope himself.

➕ G8 ✉ Calle de Cervantes 11 ☎ 91 429 92 16 🕓 Tue–Fri 9.30–2, Sat 10–2. Closed public hols, Aug 🚇 Banco de España, Antón Martín 🚌 On Paseo del Prado
💷 Inexpensive (short guided tour, in Spanish only)

COLEGIATA DE SAN ISIDRO

San Isidro is the patron saint of Madrid and, between 1885 and 1993, until the completion of the Almudena, this immense baroque church was Madrid's unofficial cathedral. Built in 1620 by Pedro Sánchez for the Jesuits, the church was commandeered by Charles III after he expelled them in San Andrés, were brought here at that time.

➕ F8 ✉ Calle Toledo 37–39 ☎ 91 369 20 37 🕓 Daily 8–12, 6.30–8.30. Closed during services 🚇 La Latina 🚌 17, 23, 35 ♿ None

GRAN VÍA

Running between the Calle Alcalá and the Plaza de España, the imposingly massive Gran Vía is one of the city's great axes; with its shops and cinemas, it is very lively and stimulating for early evening strolls. Begun in 1910 under Alfonso XII, it led to the shortening or destruction of 54 other streets. Highlights are the Grassy jewellers (corner of Calle Alcalá) and the skyscraper Telefónica buildings.

➕ F/G7 🚇 Gran Vía, Callao 🚌 44, 46, 74, 133, 146, 147, 148, 149

PLAZA DE CASCORRO

In the heart of the *barrio popular* of old Madrid, this plaza is at the top end of the fabled Rastro street market. It is a perfect place to experience the hustle and bustle of the Old Quarter on a late Sunday morning.

A portrait of Lope de Vega at his former home, Casa Museo Lope de Vega

Theatre on the Gran Vía

On the right stands Los Caracoles, a long-established seafood bar that is typical of the area.

🚩 F8 ✉ Plaza de Cascorro 🚇 La Latina, Tirso de Molina 🚌 17, 23, 35

PLAZA DE LA CEBADA

This is one of the more traditional squares, even though it no longer looks like a square. Its market, opened in 1875, was Madrid's first example of iron architecture; before its erection, bullfights were held on the site, and at the beginning of the 19th century, it was the scene of public executions.

🚩 E8 ✉ Plaza de la Cebada 🚇 La Latina, Tirso de Molina 🚌 17, 23, 35

PLAZA DEL CONDE DE BARAJAS

Looking for a special souvenir of Madrid? Visit this delightful spot on a Sunday when artists set up their stalls to sell oil paintings and watercolours. Prices range from cheap to unbelievable, but it is worth haggling. At Christmas, concerts and flamenco dancing events are also held here. It's located southwest of the Plaza Mayor between Calle de la Pasa and the Pasadizo del Panecillo.

🚩 E8 🚇 La Latína

PLAZA DE LAS CORTES

www.congreso.es

This is the home of the Congreso de los Diputados, or parliament buildings. The ceremonial entrance to the parliament is guarded by two bronze lions popularly known as Daoíz and Velarde after the heroic captains of the Napoleonic invasion. An attempted military coup took place inside the building in 1981, and was recorded on video for posterity. There are weekly guided tours.

🚩 G7 ✉ Plaza de las Cortes 🚇 Sevilla 🚌 5, 150, N5, N6

PLAZA DE LA PAJA

During Muslim rule, this pleasant little Straw Square was the site of the city's most important *zoco*, or street market; during the Middle Ages it housed aristocratic residences. Of the many palaces located here, the most

Congreso de los Diputados on Plaza de las Cortes

An outdoor café on Plaza de la Paja

notable is at No. 14, the Lasso de Castilla, the preferred residence of Catholic kings when they stayed in Madrid, sadly now extremely unpalatial in appearance.

➕ E8 ✉ Plaza de la Paja 🚇 La Latina 🚌 3, 31, 148

PLAZA DE SANTA ANA

Once occupied by the Santa Ana monastery, which was torn down during Joseph Bonaparte's rule (1808–13), the refurbished plaza is surrounded by bars and is perfect for people-watching in summer.

➕ F8 ✉ Plaza de Santa Ana 🚇 Sol, Sevilla 🚌 5, 150

PLAZA DE LA VILLA

With its small scale, this rectangular and typically Castilian square makes a pleasant change from some of the more imposing buildings in Madrid. Originally the site of an Arab street market, it is now home to three buildings in three distinct styles: the Castilian-baroque Ayuntamiento, the Casa de la Villa, designed in 1630 by Juan Gómez de Mora; the much-restored Casa de Cisneros, on the south side of the square, one of Madrid's finest examples of the plateresque style prevalent in the 16th century; and the Torre de los Lujanes, one of the few surviving monuments from the 15th century.

➕ E8 ✉ Plaza de la Villa 🚇 Sol, Ópera 🚌 3

SAN PEDRO EL VIEJO

Noteworthy principally for its 14th-century Mudéjar tower and the legends surrounding it, San Pedro stands on the site of an old mosque. In the doorway are the only coats of arms extant from the period preceding the Catholic monarchs. Part of the interior dates from the 15th century, while the rest is largely of 18th-century construction.

➕ E8 ✉ Calle Nuncio 14 ☎ 91 365 12 84 🕐 Daily 6–8pm; do not visit during Mass 🚇 La Latina, Tirso de Molina 🚫 None

Casa de Guadalajara on Plaza de Santa Ana

A Walk East from Sol

Take this walk to see the Spanish parliament and the Prado, the Botanic Gardens and Retiro Park.

DISTANCE: 6.7km (4 miles) **ALLOW:** 2–3 hours

START

PUERTA DEL SOL
✚ F7 🚇 Puerta del Sol

1 Start on the Puerta del Sol. Exit at its eastern end and walk down Calle de San Jerónimo, all the way to the Plaza de las Cortes. Continue past the south side of the Museo Thyssen-Bornemisza to the Plaza de Cánovas de Castillo.

2 Turn right down the Paseo del Prado and cross at Plaza de la Platería de Martínez. Visit the Jardín Botánico, on the south side of the Prado. Or continue along Calle de Espalter to Calle de Moreto.

3 Turn left and walk uphill, past San Jerónimo del Real, to Calle de Félipe IV. Turn right, walk up past the Casón del Buen Retiro, cross Calle de Alfonso XII and enter the Retiro Park.

END

CALLE DE ALCALÁ
✚ G7 🚇 Banco de España

7 Continue past the Plaza de las Silesa and turn sharp left down Calle de Barquillo. Follow this all the way down to Calle de Alcalá.

6 At the Plaza de Colón, turn left on Paseo de Recoletos. Cross over at the entrance to Recoletos station. On the west side of the Paseo, turn right on Calle Bárbara de Braganza.

5 At the fountain, bear left for the Puerta de Alcalá, cross Calle de Alcalá, and walk up Calle de Serrano. Pass the Archaeological Museum and turn left on Calle de Jorge Juan.

4 Stroll through the parterre gardens and up the steps at the end. When you reach the lake, turn left and follow its edge. Across the water is the dramatic Alfonso XII monument.

Shopping

AMPARO MERCERÍA
As this grand old haberdashery store confirms, stitching and mending, sewing and knitting are still popular skills in Spain. Founded back in 1861, the store retains that sense of history with a solid wooden counter, as well as selections of buttons, needles, sequins and lace.
➕ F7 ✉ Calle Marqués Viudo de Pontejos 5 ☎ 91 521 98 08 🚇 Sol

ANTIGUA CASA TALAVERA
For fine hand-painted ceramics from Talavera, Granada and Toledo. This 100-year-old establishment has both original and reproduction vases and platters with patterns that go back 1,000 years.
➕ E7 ✉ Calle de Isabel la Católica 2 ☎ 91 547 34 17 🚇 Santo Domingo

ANTIGUA PASTELERÍA DEL POZO
Spanish cakes may not be as delicate as French or Austrian pastries, but there are many with a tale to tell. This bakery dates back to 1830 and is known for its *roscones* de Reyes, a sweet bread associated with the Three Kings festival (6 January). But these rings of brioche-style bread, dotted with sugar and glazed fruits, are made on the premises year-round. Alternatively, go for the

tarts filled with pumpkin jam and custard. Closed Sun, mid Jul to end Aug.
➕ F7 ✉ Calle Pozo 8 ☎ 91 522 38 94 🚇 Sol

CASA DE DIEGO
This 150-year-old store is still the best place in Madrid to buy a real fan. They range from cheap and cheerful for use on hot days to exquisite hand-painted collector's items. Also umbrellas and walking sticks.
➕ F9 ✉ Plaza de la Puerta del Sol 12 ☎ 91 522 66 43 🚇 Sol

CASA JIMÉNEZ
For over 80 years, this family-run store has sold the finest embroidered veils and shawls. Some

WHAT'S ON OFFER?
The little specialist shops of Madrid can offer much insight into the minds of the city's inhabitants. Sometimes the shop's layout is so irrational that it is hard to know what the place is really selling. Particularly in the area around the Plaza Mayor, the district of La Latina and the area between Calle del Barco and Calle Hortaleza, just off the Gran Vía, it is worth pausing to admire off-beat window displays. These have been lovingly put together by proprietors who know they are as much a part of the urban landscape as any monument.

are works of art in their own right, and so are often framed rather than worn.
➕ E/F7 ✉ Calle de Preciados 42 ☎ 91 548 05 26 🚇 Callao, Santo Domingo

EL CORTE INGLÉS
www.elcorteingles.es
Spain's pride and joy, a department store that sells everything, combining good value and prices. Some 20 stores in Madrid, including the flagship store on Calle Preciados, just off the Puerta del Sol.
➕ F7 ✉ Calle de Preciados 1 ☎ 91 379 80 00 🚇 Sol

LA FAVORITA
The first top hats and bowler hats were sold here on the Plaza Mayor back in 1894. The shop somehow survives on more modern head gear, such as caps (*gorras*) and berets.
➕ F7 ✉ Plaza Mayor 25 ☎ 91 366 58 77 🚇 Sol

FELIX ANTIGÜEDADES
An antiques shop in the heart of the Rastro flea market where you'll find an intriguing collection of *objets d'art*, especially Oriental art and musical instruments.
➕ F9 ✉ Plaza General Vara del Rey 3 ☎ 91 528 49 30 🚇 La Latina

EL FLAMENCO VIVE
There is no doubt that flamenco lives inside

Alberto Martínez's shop, Spain's first devoted to flamenco. In addition to a good selection of music, there are books on flamenco history and much flamenco paraphernalia.
🚇 E7 ✉ Calle Conde de Lemos 7 ☎ 91 547 39 17 🔴 Opera

FNAC

Five floors of books and CDs, plus a small concert area. Also has foreign news-papers, photograph developing services and a ticket agency.
🚇 F7 ✉ Calle Preciados 28 ☎ 91 595 61 00 🔴 Callao

GALERÍAS PIQUÉR

This pleasant mall in the Rastro street market has 20 antiques shops. Try Siglo 20 for art deco, and El Estudio for Isabelline furniture and lamps.
🚇 F9 ✉ Calle Ribera de Curtidores 29 🔴 La Latina

GUITARRAS RAMÍREZ

www.guitarrasramirez.com
Since 1882, four generations of the Ramírez family have made and sold some of Spain's finest guitars for classical and flamenco music. Bought by amateurs as well as world-famous professional musicians.
🚇 F7/8 ✉ Calle de la Paz 8 ☎ 91 531 42 29 🔴 Sol

MARIANO MADRUEÑO

The Spanish drink a wide range of their own wines, as well as unusual liqueurs such as *pacharán* (sloe gin). Barrels and alembics still decorate this century-old *bodega* (wine shop), near the Monasterio de las Descalzas Reales. It's still run by the same family and you will find the staff helpful with what is an eclectic selection.
🚇 F7 ✉ Calle Postigo de San Martín 3 ☎ 91 521 19 55 🔴 Callao

SESEÑA

With a firm eye on maintaining quality control, this family establishment, dating back to 1901, specializes in capes. Pablo Picasso, Michael Jackson, and Hillary Clinton have all been customers.
🚇 F7/8 ✉ Calle de la Cruz 23 ☎ 91 531 68 40 🔴 Sol

SHOPPING AROUND

For better or worse, the retail scene in Madrid is increasingly dominated by chain stores and *centros comerciales* (shopping malls). Try and get into the back streets to visit smaller establishments. Shop assistants can be sloth-like when it comes to serving customers they don't know, and 'service with a smile' is only now starting to catch on. Larger stores are open through lunch, while smaller ones continue to close from about 1.30 to about 4.30.

STAMPS AND COINS MARKET

People meet to discuss stamps and coins under the archways of the Plaza Mayor.
🚇 F7/8 ✉ Plaza Mayor 🕐 Sunday morning 🔴 Sol

LA VIOLETA

This tiny shop could be out of a fairy tale. It specializes in an unusual sweet: real sugared violets in jars and pretty little boxes. It also sells chocolates and candied fruits, and everything is wrapped elegantly to make the ideal present.
🚇 F7 ✉ Plaza de Canalejas 6 ☎ 91 522 55 22 🔴 Sol

VIPS

www.clubvips.com
The 12 bright, bold VIPS stores around the city, convenient and impressive in size, sell books, magazines and CDs, along with food and gifts. Most are open 24 hours. Each also has a bar and restaurant.
🚇 F7 ✉ Gran Vía 43 (with branches throughout the city) ☎ 91 275 20 93 🔴 Callao

ZARA

Now a household name around the world, Spanish chain Zara has five main street stores in Madrid, offering stylish mainstream fashion for men and women at down-to-earth prices.
🚇 F7 ✉ Gran Vía 32 ☎ 91 522 97 27 🔴 Gran Vía

Entertainment and Nightlife

ARCO DE CUCHILLEROS

At this *tablao flamenco*, close to the Plaza Mayor, top flamenco dancers and singers have performed for nearly 50 years. Rather than a theatre or nightclub, this is more a bar with entertainment, so have a drink and watch the action between 9pm and 2am. Closed Monday.

➕ E8 ✉ Calle Cuchilleros 7 ☎ 91 364 02 63 🚇 Sol

BERLIN CABARET 1930

www.berlincabaret.com
The Spanish still love magic tricks, as well as the usual risqué song and dance, drag shows and high-kicking chorus lines. Expect lots of red velvet and a happy crowd. But, be warned: shows at this café theatre often start as late as 1am.

➕ E8 ✉ Costanilla de San Pedro 11 ☎ 91 366 20 34 🚇 La Latina, Ópera

LA BOCA DEL LOBO

'The Jaws of the Wolf' is a lively dance bar where the music can be anything from hip-hop to rock 'n' roll, depending on the DJ. Dark, smoky atmosphere. Open from 10pm till late.

➕ G7/8 ✉ Calle Echegaray 11 ☎ 91 429 70 13 🚇 Sevilla

THE BOURBON CAFÉ

www.thebourboncafe.net
Choose between the disco and the live bands at this youth-oriented club. The disco has themed nights, from Mexican to hip-hop; live bands range from rock and jazz to Latin and flamenco pop. Out-and-out fun, with lots of loud music and fast food from hamburgers to pizzas, served till 11pm.

🏳 F7 ✉ Calle Carrera de San Jerónimo 5 ☎ 91 532 58 57 🚇 Sol

CAFÉ CENTRAL

One of the best jazz venues in Europe. There are performances every night mainly from Spanish, but sometimes foreign, musicians.

➕ F8 ✉ Plaza del Ángel 10 ☎ 91 369 41 43 🕐 Daily 10.30pm 🚇 Sevilla, Antón Martín, Sol

CAFÉ POPULART

Live music every day—jazz, blues and swing—in a comfortable environment with intelligent conversation.

➕ G8 ✉ Calle Huertas 22 ☎ 91 429 84 07 🚇 Antón Martín

RAVE ON

The limitless capacity of *madrileños* for having fun has made Madrid a dance club owner's dream. The city is the undisputed European nightlife capital, and the night begins and ends very late indeed.

LAS CARBONERAS

Madrid's newest flamenco club is already rated by *aficionados* for its quality acts. The show begins around 11pm, but arrive earlier if you want to be sure of a seat.

➕ E8 ✉ Calle del Conde de Miranda 1 ☎ 91 542 86 77 🚇 Sol

CASA PATAS

The best-known of Madrid's flamenco *tablaos* is a little touristy, but none the less enjoyable. Live midnight performances, more frequent in May.

➕ F8 ✉ Calle Cañizares 10 ☎ 91 369 15 74/04 96 🕐 Thu–Sat midnight 🚇 Tirso de Molina, Antón Martín

CERVECERÍA ALEMANA

One of the city's most popular bars. A good meeting place in the Santa Ana district.

➕ F8 ✉ Plaza de Santa Ana 6 ☎ 91 429 70 33 🚇 Antón Martín

LE COCK

Round off the evening with a cocktail or two beneath the glass roof of this tastefully decorated late-night bar.

➕ G7 ✉ Calle Reina 16 ☎ 91 532 28 26 🚇 Banco de España

LA COQUETTE

The only Madrid bar dedicated exclusively to blues is very 1960s.

ENTERTAINMENT AND NIGHTLIFE

⊞ E/F7 ⊠ Calle de las Hileras 14 Ⓜ Opera

LA CORRALA

La Corrala is used for open-air *zarzuela* performances in summer.
⊞ F9 ⊠ Calle Tribulete 12 ☎ No phone Ⓜ Lavapiés

LOS GABRIELES

Decorated throughout with stunning *azulejos* (tiles). Around 11pm tables are packed away and it becomes more like a nightclub, with a DJ at weekends. Flamenco on Tuesday evenings.
⊞ G8 ⊠ Calle Echegaray 17 ☎ 91 429 62 61 Ⓜ Sevilla

GLASS BAR

In the lobby of the Hotel Urban, this has been voted as the cool place by trendy magazines. Lots of glass, expensive cocktails and music that ranges from disco and soul to funky and pop.
⊞ G7 ⊠ Carrera de San Jerónimo 34 ⊙ Daily 11am–3am ☎ 91 787 77 70 Ⓜ Sol, Antón Martín

JOY ESLAVA (MADRID)

Plush, though not forbiddingly stylish, club in an 1850s theatre. The central location attracts a diverse clientele.
⊞ F7 ⊠ Calle Arenal 11 ☎ 91 366 37 33 Ⓜ Ópera

PALACIO DE GAVIRIA

One of Madrid's more remarkable night-time locations. An 1851 palace, with fixtures and furniture generally intact, it reopened in 1981 as a nightspot. With its grand staircase entrance and 14 halls, it is well worth checking out.
⊞ F7 ⊠ Calle Arenal 9 ☎ 91 526 60 69 Ⓜ Sol

THE PENTHOUSE LOUNGE AND TERRACE

For spectacular views and equally spectacular cocktails, such as their very own Lavender Margarita, head to the top floor of the hip new ME Madrid Reina Victoria Hotel.
⊞ F8 ⊠ ME Madrid Hotel Plaza de Santa Ana 14 ⊙ Wed–Sat 9pm–4am, Sun 5–midnight ☎ 91 701 60 00 Ⓜ Sol, Antón Martín

TEATRO MONUMENTAL

The place where classical concerts are recorded for broadcast by the Spanish Radio and Televison Orchestra and Choir.

ZARZUELA

In the words of Edmundo de Amici, writing in 1870, the *zarzuela* is 'a piece of music somewhere between comedy and melodrama, between opera and vaudeville, with prose and verse, both recited and sung, serious and lighthearted, a very Spanish and very entertaining musical form.' Among audiences of a certain age, it remains as popular as ever.

⊞ G8 ⊠ Calle Atocha 65 ☎ 91 429 12 81/902 33 22 11 Ⓜ Antón Martín

TEATRO DE LA ZARZUELA

Light opera called 'zarzuela' is particularly popular with the older generation in Madrid. Even if you don't speak Spanish, the farcical plots are so simple that anyone can understand them. And the music and singing are top class. Enjoy it at this glitzy 150-year-old theatre.
⊞ G7 ⊠ Jovellanos 4 ☎ 91 524 54 00 ⊙ Varies, check schedule Ⓜ Antón Martín

TORRES BERMEJAS

www.torresbermejas.com
For over 40 years, this restaurant and club has hosted some of the most famous flamenco singers and dancers in the world. The setting is reminiscent of the Alhambra palace in Granada. Eat traditional Spanish dishes, such as paella, and then enjoy the show. More for tourists than locals.
⊞ F7 ⊠ Mesonero Romanos 11 ☎ 91 532 33 22 Ⓜ Callao

VIVA MADRID

The tiled *azulejo* frontage of Viva Madrid bar has been photographed for a thousand guide books.
⊞ G8 ⊠ Calle Manuel Fernández y González 7 ☎ 91 429 36 40 Ⓜ Antón Martín

Restaurants

PRICES

Prices are approximate, based on a 3-course meal for one person.
€€€   over €45
€€   €25–€45
€   under €25

BOTÍN (€€)

Botín first opened its doors in 1725, making it, according to the *Guinness Book of Records*, the world's oldest restaurant. Suckling pig, roasted in a wood-fired oven, is the Castillian special dish.
🚇 E8 ✉ Calle Cuchilleros 17 ☎ 91 366 42 17 🚇 La Latina

LOS CARACOLES (€)

How authentic do you want? This is all about snails: casseroled, with lots of garlic. Wash them down with a glass of draft vermouth. Eat standing up; feel like a local.
🚇 E9 ✉ Calle de Toledo 106 ☎ 91 366 42 46 🕐 Tue–Sat, 9am–11pm, Sun till 7.30pm 🚇 Puerta de Toledo

CASA ALBERTO (€)

Characterful restaurant, founded in 1827, at the back of a bar that serves terrific tapas. It's full of bull-fighting memorabilia. The ham croquettes and oxtail are recommended.
🚇 G8 ✉ Calle Huertas 18 ☎ 91 429 93 56 🕐 Closed Sun night, Mon and 2 weeks in Aug 🚇 Antón Martín

CASA LABRA (€)

The Spanish Socialist Party was founded here in 1879, just 19 years after the bar was established, and Casa Labra has been producing typically *madrileño* tapas ever since. Cod croquettes are a house special.
🚇 F7 ✉ Calle Tetuán 12 ☎ 91 532 14 05 🚇 Sol

CERVECERÍA CERVANTES (€)

Packed with locals looking for the best fish and seafood tapas in town. Just point at what you fancy. The *tostada de gamba*, hot shrimps in aioli on toast, are quite delicious.
🚇 G8 ✉ Plaza de Jesús, 7 ☎ 91 429 60 93 🕐 Daily 12.30–5pm, 7.15–11.45pm. Closed Sun evening 🚇 Antón Martín

CHOCOLATERÍA SAN GINÉS (€)

Flashy, big and extremely

NEW TASTES

For historical and geographical reasons, both Latin American and North African cuisine are increasingly popular on Madrid's hitherto fairly conservative culinary scene. The menus can be as incomprehensible to Spaniards as to any visitor. The best bet is to see what others are eating and order what looks appealing.

busy, especially in winter. Three minutes from Sol.
🚇 F7 ✉ Pasaje de San Ginés 5 ☎ 91 365 65 46 🚇 Sol, Ópera

ERROTA-ZAR (€€)

Opposite the Teatro de la Zarzuela, this has been one of the city's most authentic Basque restaurants for over 20 years. Specialties include fried fresh anchovies, tartare of bonito and a variety of traditional dishes using hake, string beans or mushrooms. As well as local cheeses, there are good desserts, such as chocolate cake and ice cream. The wine cellar has over 10,000 bottles.
🚇 G7 ✉ Calle Jovellanos 3 (first floor) ☎ 91 531 25 64 🕐 Daily; closed Sun 🚇 Banco de España

LA ESQUINA DEL CAFÉ (€)

Tiny corner café that is known for its yummy desserts, such as tiramisu and chocolate cake. Ideal for a break from tapas, with a *café con leche* (coffee with hot milk).
🚇 G8 ✉ Calle de Jesús 10 ☎ 91 369 30 84 🕐 Daily 12.30–5pm, 7.15–11.45pm. Closed Sun evening 🚇 Antón Martín

LHARDY (€€–€€€)

One of the city's classier restaurants and a local institution. The good range of fairly pricey tapas downstairs includes consommé, croquettes,

Russian salad on bread and, in summer, Madrid's best gazpacho. There is also a delicatessen.

F7 ⊠ Calle Carrera de San Jerónimo 8 ☎ 91 521 33 85 🕐 Closed dinner, Sun, public hols 🚇 Sol

POSADA DE LA VILLA (€€€)

www.posadadelavilla.com
The building just off the Plaza Mayor dates back to 1642 and the atmosphere and dishes are about as traditional as you can get. This is the place to order Madrid oven-roast lamb and *cocido* (Madrid's favourite stew, order 24 hours in advance). Locals are as happy here as tourists.

E8 ⊠ Cava Baja 9 ☎ 91 366 18 60 🕐 Closed Sun dinner 🚇 Latina, Tirso de Molina, Sol

RESTAURANTE MOAÑA (€€€)

In an old-fashioned and rather formal setting, chef Francisco Romero Vieite reworks traditional Galician recipes for fish and seafood. Choose from scallops, lobster, cod and more. Wide range of Galician wines.

E7 ⊠ Calle de las Hileras 4 ☎ 91 548 29 14 🕐 Closed Sun, dinner 🚇 Ópera

TABERNA DE ANTONIO SÁNCHEZ (€)

The best-conserved of all the tapas bars pays homage to the bullfighting family that has run it since 1830. Displays on bullfighting make the distinctive setting as fascinating as the tapas.

F8 ⊠ Calle Mesón de Paredes 13 ☎ 91 539 78 26 🚇 Tirso de Molina

TABERNA MACEIRA (€)

Join the *madrileños* standing outside and wait for a table in this popular Galician-style haunt. Menus are on artists' palettes, the music is Galician bagpipes and the helpings are large: *pulpo* (octopus), *patatas bravas* (spicy potatoes) and jugs of sangría. Cramped, noisy, good value and good fun. Cash only, no reservations.

G8 ⊠ Calle de las Huertas 66 ☎ 91 429 58 18 🕐 Daily 12–12 🚇 Antón Martín

MADRID GASTRONOMY

Madrid and its region have a distinctive style of cooking, which is plain, straightforward and tasty. *Asado* means roast, and there's nothing better than roast lamb or kid from a wood-fired oven. The other major local favourite is *cocido*, a stew with meat, chick peas and vegetables. These are cooked together in a clay pot, right in the fireplace. Match these with the regional red wines made from Tempranillo grapes.

LA TAURINA (€)

This is a shrine to bullfighting with everything from bulls' heads and capes to sequined matador costumes and tiled murals of bullfights. But it is also a great place for tapas and heartier home-cooked Andalucian dishes, such as ox tail, gazpacho, black pudding, squid, tortilla and anchovies.

F7 ⊠ Carrera de San Jerónimo 5 ☎ 91 531 39 69 🕐 Daily 🚇 Sol

VINOTECA BARBECHERA (€)

www.vinoteca-barbechera.com
Part of a successful chain of wine bars, this is a good place to see modern Madrid at play. Good range of snacks: platters of smoked tuna and trout, rolls stuffed with chorizo, ham or anchovies, crêpes for dessert, plus a wide range of wines by the glass from Spain and abroad. Six venues in Madrid, including one on Plaza de Santa Ana.

G8 ⊠ Calle del Príncipe 27 ☎ 91 420 04 78 🕐 Daily 10am–midnight 🚇 Antón Martín, Sol

VIUDA DE VACAS (€)

Madrileños like to bring overseas visitors here for traditional Spanish cooking amid *azulejo* tiles and wooden tables.

E8 ⊠ Calle Cava Alta 23 ☎ 91 366 58 47 🕐 Closed Sun night Aug 🚇 La Latina

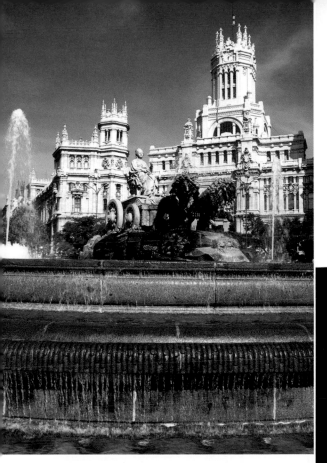

With one of the world's most famous art museums and one of the world's great urban parks, this part of Madrid is a magnet for visitors. But don't miss the Real Fábrica de Tapices, the tapestry factory, where tradition rules.

Jerónimos and the East

HIGHLIGHTS

- *Las Meninas*, Velázquez
- Goya's 'dark paintings'
- *The 2nd of May, The 3rd of May, Las Majas*, Goya
- *The Holy Family*, Raphael
- *The Bacchanal, Emperor Charles V in Mühlberg*, Titian
- *The Garden of Delights*, Bosch
- *The Triumph of Death*, Brueghel
- *Self Portrait*, Dürer
- *David and Goliath*, Caravaggio
- *The Three Graces*, Rubens

TIPS

- Weekends are always crowded; plan to go first thing in the morning, or at the end of the day.
- When renovated, the Casón del Buen Retiro will house the Prado's collection of 19th-century art.

The city's pride in the magnificent Prado is justified. With its Goyas, El Grecos and other masterpieces, it is undoubtedly one of the great art museums of the world.

Brief history The neoclassical building, completed by Juan de Villanueva in 1785, was conceived by Charles III as a centre for the study of natural sciences. After Napoléon's troops damaged it during the Spanish Wars of Succession, it was restored by Fernando VII as a home for the royal collection of paintings and sculptures and opened as a museum in November 1819. It is unequalled in the world, with a collection numbering 7,000 pictures, of which around 1,500 are on display at any given time; there are 115 Goyas, 83 works by Rubens, 50 by Velázquez, 40 Brueghels, 36 Titians, 32 El Grecos and 20 Zurbaráns. With the

The Museo del Prado has over 1,500 paintings on diplay, but don't miss those by Goya, Velázquez, El Greco, Brueghel and Titian

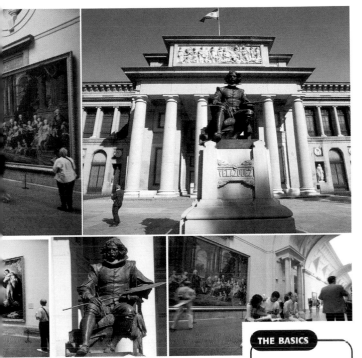

opening of the extension in 2007, the museum gains much-needed space for temporary exhibitions. Like all great museums, the Prado is best appreciated in more than one visit.

Velázquez and Goya Do not leave the Prado without seeing Velázquez's masterpiece, *Las Meninas*, widely considered technically the finest painting in the world. Goya's *Majas*—two paintings believed to be of the Duchess of Alba, one naked, one clothed—positively beckon the spectator into the picture, Madrid's seductive answer to the Mona Lisa. Goya's *pinturas negras*—among them *Saturn Devouring One of his Sons* and *Half-Drowned Dog*—are obviously the work of a man whose sanity is in decline. At once grotesque, disturbing and breathtaking, they are unique.

THE BASICS

✚ H8
✉ Paseo del Prado
🕐 Tue–Sun 9 0, public hols 9–2
☎ 91 330 28 00
🍴 Restaurant, café
Ⓜ Banco de España, Atocha
🚌 9, 10, 14, 19, 27, 34, 37, 45
🚉 Atocha, Recoletos
♿ Moderate. Free under 18, over 65, Sun
❓ Abono Paseo del Arte/Bonoarte gives reduced fee entry to the Prado, Reina Sofía and Thyssen-Bornemisza

Small enough to be welcoming, but large enough to get pleasantly lost in, the Retiro will linger in your memory, particularly if you see it in late spring or early autumn when its colours are most vivid.

History On a sunny Sunday afternoon, the whole city seems drawn to the Retiro park, 1.2sq km (0.5sq miles) in the city centre, whose name translates as 'retreat'. Originally thickly wooded and once a hunting ground for Philip II, the Retiro was the brainchild of the Duke of Olivares, who designed it in the 1630s for Philip IV as part of the Buen Retiro Palace - a complex of royal buildings and immense formal gardens that inspired Louis XIV at Versailles. It was used until the time of Charles III, who partially opened it to the public in the 1770s. Most of the palace was destroyed during the Napoleonic Wars.

A walk in the park Use the entrance on Calle Alfonso XII, opposite the Casón del Buen Retiro. Walk through the parterre gardens and up the steps along a broad, shady avenue to the lake. If you want to take a boat out, head left around the lake; opposite you is a statue of Alfonso XII, a popular spot to soak up the sun. Otherwise, turn right and follow the Paseo de Republica de Cuba. From here, you can take one of many paths leading to the Palacio de Cristal (Glass Palace), the Retiro's loveliest building. Constructed in 1886, it is one of several exhibition spaces within the park. At the southern end of the park is La Rosaleda (the Rose Garden), in full glory in May.

THE BASICS

H7–J8

Calle Alcalá, Alfonso XII, Avenida de Menedez Pelayo, Paseo de la Reina Cristina

May–Sep 6am–midnight, Oct–Apr 6am–10pm

Terrazas

Retiro, Atocha, Ibiza

2, 14, 19, 20, 26, 28, 68, 69

Atocha, Retiro

HIGHLIGHTS

● Palacio de Cristal
● Artichoke Fountain in the Rose Garden
● Cecilio Rodríguez Gardens
● Velázquez Palace
● Statue of Alfonso XII
● Lake
● Fallen Angel statue
● 400-year-old cypress tree near Philip IV entrance
● Philip IV parterre
● Observatory (1790)
● Free band concerts from May to October
● Puppet shows for children on Sunday

Plaza de la Cibeles

The fountain of La Cibeles, on Plaza de la Cibeles (left and right)

THE BASICS

➕ H7
✉ Plaza de la Cibeles
🚇 Banco de España
🚌 5, 9, 10, 14, 20, 27, 34, 45, 51, 53
🚊 Atocha, Recoletos

HIGHLIGHTS

● Post Office
● Gardens of Palacio de Linares
● Façade of Bank of Spain building
● Robert Michel's lions
● Newspaper stand on Paseo del Prado

Despite the constant traffic, this plaza, a sheer mass of stone around a dramatic statue of the fertility goddess, La Cibeles, is Madrid's most overwhelming square.

Cars pass by Seated imperiously at one of Madrid's busiest intersections, the goddess and her marble fountain were erected according to instructions from Charles III (1716–88). The main statue is by Francisco Gutiérrez and the lions, Hipponomes and Atlanta, drawing the goddess' chariot, are by Robert Michel. Originally at the corner of the square, the statue was finally completed in 1792 and moved in 1895, at which date the cherubim were added.

Around the Plaza The enormous wedding-cake look-alike on the southeastern side of the square is one of Madrid's most imposing buildings. It was designed by Antonio Palacios in 1904, its painstakingly worked façade reminiscent of Viennese style. Designed by Antonio Palacios in 1904 to be the Palacio de Comunicaciones (Central Post Office), it was dubbed by local wits as Our Lady of Communications, as if it were a cathedral. The plan is to make this the new City Hall.

The Palacio de Linares The real treasure of the Plaza de la Cibeles is the elaborately decorated Palacio de Linares. It was designed in 1872, and restored and opened in 1992 as the Casa de América. It now showcases exhibits about Latin American visual arts.

The five-arched Puerta de Alcalá is a symbol of Madrid

Puerta de Alcalá

If you are travelling from the airport by taxi to Madrid's centre, this gateway is one of the first things you will see. It is perhaps the city's most powerful emblem, particularly when lit at night.

Neoclassical symbol Listed as a National Monument, the Puerta de Alcalá in the Plaza de la Independencia is one of the great symbols of Madrid. It is perhaps the city's finest example of the neoclassical architecture that came as a reaction to previous baroque excesses. Commissioned by Charles III, who was to be responsible for so much of the city's architectural transformation, it was designed by Francisco Sabatini in 1778 as the main entrance to the Court. Best appreciated when floodlit at night, the Puerta de Alcalá stands in the middle of an immense traffic junction, so it can be admired only from a distance.

Design Made up of five arches of granite and stone, the statue has 10 columns similar to those by Michelangelo for the Capitol in Rome—facing east and crowned with Ionic capitals. Three central archways are flanked by two smaller ones. The lion heads in the middle of the three higher arches are the work of Robert Michel, and the cherubim, the trophies and the coat of arms that surmount the statue are by Francisco Gutiérrez. You can still see the bullet marks from the 1921 assassination attempt on Eduardo Dato, President of Madrid's Council of Ministers, on the north side of the statue. Luckily, a Madrid Town Council proposal to paint parts of the *puerta* white was rejected.

THE BASICS

🚇 H7
✉ Plaza de la Independencia
🚇 Retiro
🚌 9, 19, 15, 20, 28, 51, 52, 74
🚋 Recoletos

HIGHLIGHTS

● Views of the monument at night when floodlit
● The lion heads designed by Robert Michel
● Bullet holes dating from a 1921 assassination attempt

More to See

CASÓN DEL BUEN RETIRO

www.museoprado.es

This was originally the ballroom of the Buen Retiro Royal Palace, a building destroyed by Napoleonic troops but rebuilt by Charles III, who had the vault decorated with frescoes. When the extensive renovations are finished, this will house the Prado's collection of 19th-century art.

➕ H8 ✉ Calle Alfonso XII 68 🚇 Retiro, Banco de España 🚌 19

ESTACIÓN DE ATOCHA

Some 2,000sq m (21,530sq ft) of indoor tropical garden can be found inside this impressive late 19th-century wrought-iron station canopy by Alberto del Palacio. The cylindrical glass tower next to the station is a monument to the 191 victims of the 11 March, 2004 bomb attacks on Madrid trains.

➕ H9 ✉ Plaza del Emperador Carlos V ☎ 91 527 31 60 🚇 Atocha 🚌 14, 27, 34, 37, 45 ♿ Few

JARDÍN BOTÁNICO

www.rjb.csic.es

These peaceful gardens are the result of overseas expeditions in search of interesting species dating back to the 18th century. The plants and trees are carefully classified and laid out along geometrical walkways.

➕ H8 ✉ Plaza de Murillo 2 🕐 Daily from 10am; closing varies with season 🚇 Atocha 🚌 10, 14, 27, 34, 37, 45 💰 Inexpensive

JARDINES DEL DESCUBRIMIENTO

Typical of Madrid town planning of the 1970s, these sculpture gardens in the Plaza de Colón were built to celebrate Spain's role in the discovery of the New World. The gardens are dominated by an 1892 Jerónimo Suñol statue of Christopher Columbus, but it is the wonderful Joaquín Vaquero Turcios sculptures from 1977 that are the real highlight. The three statues represent Columbus' three ships—the *Pinta*, the *Niña* and the *Santa María*—as they sail across the Atlantic in 1492 towards the fourth statue, the New

Estación de Atocha

Casón del Buen Retiro

World. You can best appreciate the effect by standing well back. Underneath the gardens is the Centro Cultural de la Villa de Madrid.

✛ H6 ✉ Plaza de Colón Ⓜ Recoletos
🚌 1, 5, 9, 14, 19, 21, 27, 37, 45, 51, 53, 74, 89

PLAZA DE LA LEALTAD

A stone's throw from the Prado, this elegant, semicircular plaza dominated by the Ritz Hotel has an obelisk in the middle to the memory of those who died at the hands of Napoleonic troops on 3 May 1808. Their ashes are kept in an urn at the base of the monument. The Madrid Stock Exchange was built here in 1884, in a neoclassical design that neatly echoes the Prado.

✛ H7 ✉ Plaza de la Lealtad Ⓜ Banco de España 🚌 10, 14, 27, 34, 37, 45

REAL FÁBRICA DE TAPICES

www.realfabricadetapices.com
The centuries-old craft of creating tapestries and carpets continues in the Royal Tapestry Factory. The looms still hum as they did back in the 18th century, when the Flemish van der Goten family founded the works. On the tour (about 40 minutes) you learn that many of the original designs were created by Goya and other famous artists, and that it can take four months to finish one square metre.

✛ J9 ✉ Calle de Fuenterrabía 2 ☎ 91 434 05 50 🕐 Mon–Fri 10–2. Closed Sat, Sun, Holy Week, Aug Ⓜ Atocha, Menéndez Pelayo 🚌 14, 24, 26, 32, 37, 54, 57, 140, 141 💶 Inexpensive ♿ None

SAN JERÓNIMO EL REAL

Iglesia de San Jerónimo el Real, Madrid's society church, wedged at the side of the Prado, was built back in 1505, but over the centuries renovations included several controversial neo-Gothic additions. The steps at the entrance on Calle Alarcón, for example, were built especially for the wedding of Alfonso XIII and his queen, Victoria Eugenia, in 1906.

✛ H8 ✉ Calle Ruíz de Alarcón 19 ☎ 91 420 30 78 🕐 Jul–Sep 10–1pm, 6–8.30pm; Oct–Jun 10–1.30pm, 5–8.30pm Ⓜ Atocha, Banco de España 🚌 Free ♿ Difficult

Craftspeople at work in the Royal Tapestry Factory

Shopping

CORONEL TAPIOCCA

www.coroneltapiocca.com
A chain aimed at the modern-day adventurer, selling everything from rucksacks, trousers and fishing gear to camping and hunting equipment, plus useful things, such as torches. Designed for comfort, the clothes also appeal to the urban dweller who wants to look sporty.

➕ H9 ✉ Glorieta del Emperador Carlos V ☎ 91 467 29 74 Ⓜ Atocha

FABENDI

Established for over 30 years, this is a shop that locals head for when they want something—anything—in leather: leather and suede coats, jackets, trousers and suits. A wide choice.

➕ K9 ✉ Avenida del Mediterráneo 5 ☎ 91 552 24 14 Ⓜ Menéndez Pelayo

GALERÍA DE ARTE VICTORIA HIDALGO

www.victoriahidalgo.com
A step away from the Prado museum. Ever since 1998, this gallery has shown paintings and sculptures by living artists. Changing exhibits.

➕ H8 ✉ Calle de Ruiz de Alarcón 27 ☎ 91 429 56 65 Ⓜ Banco de España

IMAGINARIUM

Much more than a children's toy shop, this is all about what the name promises: imagination. From musical toys to dolls, the idea is to encourage children to have fun, in a creative, yet educational way. Think inflatable city—with skyscrapers.

➕ H9 ✉ Plaza del Emperador Carlos V ☎ 91 506 21 23 Ⓜ Atocha

NATURA SELECTION

Dedicated to arts and crafts, plus clothes from South America, Asia and Africa. All are one of a kind, with scarves and bags, lamps and gloves—all made of natural materials such as cotton, silk and leather.

➕ H9 ✉ Plaza del Emperador Carlos V ☎ 91 467 21 28 Ⓜ Atocha

ORDENATRIUM

www.ordenatrium.com
The idea of a shop selling only storage items sounds dull until you visit this inventive store. From hangers and tie racks to cleverly designed luggage and ideas for storing shoes.

➕ K6 ✉ Calle de Jorge Juan 69 ☎ 91 781 11 42 Ⓜ Goya

PERFUMERÍA ALVAREZ GOMEZ

www.alvarezgomez.com
There are branches of this long-established perfumery all over Madrid. They sell a huge range of cosmetics and scents, but mostly their own delicate, flowery fragrances and colognes, beautifully bottled and excellent value.

➕ H6 ✉ Calle de Serrano 14 ☎ 91 431 16 56 Ⓜ Retiro

PIEL DE TORO

www.pieldetoro.com
Famous for must-have T-shirts, with a design that looks like a bull, and also like the outline of Spain. Bought by surfers as well as non-sporty fashionistas. Almost directly opposite the Jardín Botánico. This is a trendy Madrid souvenir shop for adults as well as children.

➕ H8 ✉ Paseo del Prado 42 ☎ 91 360 07 52 Ⓜ Atocha

MUSEO DEL PRADO

The museum's excellent Palacios y Museos shop is a great place to find quality souvenirs. As well as fine reproductions of famous works, there are silk scarves and blouses, pictures and chocolates, ties and jewellery.

➕ H8 ✉ Paseo del Prado ☎ 91 330 29 00 Ⓜ Banco de España

WHERE TO GO

Madrid's amazing array of antique shops are in three main areas: the *barrio* Salamanca, around the Calle del Prado and Santa Ana, and around the Rastro, particularly down the Calle Ribera de Curtidores—the most likely source for bargains. Many shops do not specialize in any particular goods, but sell a broad selection of merchandise.

Entertainment and Nightlife

DISCOTECA AZÚCAR

Even if you cannot dance the salsa, you can have lessons every night at this popular Latin American club where the music is persistent and the crowd is fun, with many clubbers from South America.
➕ J9 ✉ Paseo Reina Cristina 7 ☎ 91 501 61 07 ⏰ Daily 11pm–6am, Fri–Sat 11.30–6.30 Ⓜ Atocha

FLORIDA PARK

www.floridapark.net
Just inside the gates on the eastern side of the Retiro Park, Florida Park has long been a popular destination for out-of-town visitors. With a restaurant, dance floor and stage, this suits those who enjoy a show and dancing late into the night.
➕ J7 ✉ Avenida de

Menéndez Pelayo (at Ibiza) ☎ 91 573 78 04 ⏰ Daily 9pm–3am. Closed Sun, Mon Ⓜ Ibiza

KAPITAL

www.grupo-kapital.com
With seven floors of dancing, this could be the

MADRID BY NIGHT

With almost 4,000 places to have a drink, Madrid can claim to be Europe's finest city for sheer variety of late-night options—sometimes very late indeed. Main bar areas in the centre are the start of the Paseo de la Castellana (sophisticated), Malasaña (thoroughly unsophisticated), La Latina and Santa Ana (somewhere in between), and Chueca (gay).

biggest club in Madrid. There is everything from salsa, house and karaoke to R'n'B, go-go dancers and a cinema. The great attraction in summer is the rooftop terrace. Although teenagers dominate in the early evening, grown-ups flood in later on, when the dress code is smart-casual.
➕ H9 ✉ Calle de Atocha 125 ☎ 91 420 29 06 ⏰ Fri, Sat 5.30pm–10.30pm; Thu–Sun midnight–6am Ⓜ Atocha

EL RETIRO

Sundays in the park (▷ 72) are famous for the entertainers and musicians who keep old and young amused. Outstanding are the summer concerts, called Veranos de la Villa.

Restaurants

PRICES

Prices are approximate, based on a 3-course meal for one person.
€€€   over €45
€€   €25–€45
€   under €25

AC PALACIO DEL RETIRO (€€€)

www.ac-hotels.com
Chef David Herranz takes hotel dining to a new level in this smart,

contemporary setting. Known for his delicate touch, and for giving a modern twist to traditional Mediterranean dishes. Outstanding wine list.
➕ H7 ✉ Calle de Alfonso XII 14 ☎ 91 523 74 60 ⏰ Daily lunch, dinner Ⓜ Retiro, Banco de España

BALZAC (€€€)

Close to the Prado, this is a special occasion restaurant where service comes with gleaming silverware.

Once known for its Basque cuisine, the menu is now more modern-Mediterranean and sometimes rather daring: pigeon with fruit compote, foie gras salad, pears poached in port. Exceptional wine cellar.
➕ H8 ✉ Calle de Moreto 7 ☎ 91 420 01 77 ⏰ Closed Sat lunch, Sun Ⓜ Retiro

LA CASTELA (€)

www.lacastela.com
A local favourite, this

typical *taberna* is part tapas bar for Spanish snacks, part dining room with an international menu.
✚ K7 ✉ Calle del Doctor Castelo 22 ☎ 91 574 00 15 🕐 Daily 2–4, 9–midnight. Closed Sun 🚇 Ibiza, Príncipe de Vergara

LA GAMELLA (€€€)

www.lagamella.com
On the first floor of a splendid old building that was the birthplace of Spanish philosopher José Ortega y Gasset, this small American-owned restaurant is across from the Retiro. Here 'fusion' cooking mixes Spanish and American at the top end of the range: steak tartare with a shot of Jack Daniels, a classic Caesar salad and proper burgers.
✚ H7 ✉ Calle de Alfonso XII 4 ☎ 91 532 45 09 🕐 Daily 1.30pm–4, 9–late. Closed Sat lunch, Sun 🚇 Retiro

LA HOJA (€)

www.lahoja.es
Free-range chicken is the base of all the cooking at this straightforward, family-run restaurant, where the emphasis is on Asturian-style recipes.
✚ K7 ✉ Calle del Doctor Castelo 48 ☎ 91 409 25 22 🕐 Daily 1pm–midnight. Closed Sun, Mon dinner 🚇 Ibiza, Príncipe de Vergara

RESTAURANTE VIRIDIANA (€€€)

www.restauranteviridiana.com

At one of Madrid's finest restaurants, Abraham García is known as a character, but he is also a very fine cook, preparing complex modern dishes using traditional and high-quality Spanish produce. The wine list is one of the best in the city.
✚ H7 ✉ Calle de Juan de Mena 14 ☎ 91 531 10 39 🕐 Daily 1.30–4, 8.30–midnight 🚇 Banco de España, Retiro

RITZ HOTEL (€€)

www.ritzmadrid.com
What could be more traditional than tea at the Ritz? In the Lobby Bar, listen to the pianist, harpist or classical Spanish guitarist as you

TAPAS

The tapa, a snack to accompany your drink, is a part of Spanish culture. It started in the 18th century when Carlos III insisted that his entourage cover their wine with a plate of food to keep dust from getting into it (*tapa* means 'lid'). Many bars no longer display their wares, which can make it hard to order; it's easier when the tapas are kept behind glass so you can see them before buying. Pay before leaving, rather than on a round-by-round basis. Many *cervecerías* (late-night bars) sell tapas and make an atmospheric venue for a night-time snack.

sip tea and nibble elegant sandwiches, pastries and scones. In summer, the experience is even nicer—take a white wicker chair in the garden for lunch, tapas or dinner.
✚ H7 ✉ Plaza de la Lealtad 5 ☎ 91 701 67 67 🕐 Daily 4.30–7pm 🚇 Banco de España

SULA (€€–€€€)

www.sula.es
Star chef Quique Dacosta's ultra-cool geometric bar, restaurant and luxury gourmet food shop is geared to leading-edge fashion food. Every dish—from imaginative salads, carpaccios and the finest Spanish hams to pastas and desserts—is a treat for the eye. The wine cellar is one of the city's best.
✚ J6 ✉ Calle de Jorge Juan 33 ☎ 91 781 61 97 🕐 Daily 12–12 🚇 Velázquez, Retiro

TRATTORIA SANT'ARCANGELO (€€)

In a semi-basement, just a few steps from the Prado and the Jardín Botánico, this is rated as one of Madrid's best, as well as most authentic Italian restaurants. Carefully prepared dishes include crispy pizzas, spaghetti with a rich seafood sauce and tiramisu.
✚ H8 ✉ Calle de Moreto 15 ☎ 91 369 10 93 🕐 Daily 🚇 Banco de España

Although it is known as the city's gay area, Chueca is open to all, with a variety of fun restaurants. Then there is Malasaña; considered clubland by many youngsters, this area is being gentrified.

Chueca and the North

Calle Carbonero y S
Calle de Grijalba

PASEO DE LA CASTELLANA

Calle Maestro VITRU

Ministerio
Trabajo y
S Social

Ministerio
de Medio
Ambiente

Calle de Cristóbal Bordiú

Museo de Geología

**Botero
Statues**

CALLE DE RÍOS ROSAS

RÍOS ROSAS

Cano

Ponzano

Calle de

Fuente

Espronceda

Plaza de San Juan
de la Cruz

Museo Nacional
de Ciencias
Naturales y
Zoología

**Sala del Canal
de Isabel II**

*Parque
Santa
Engracia*

Ríos
Rosas

Calle de

Alonso

Hoz

Ministerio
Defensa

Bretón

Modesto

de

los

Zurbano

Herreros

Monumento
de Isabel
La Católica

CALLE

CHAMBERÍ

CALLE DE SANTA ENGRACIA

Calle

de

CALLE

Canal

JOSÉ

ABASCAL

Plaza Dr
Marañón

CALLE

Alonso
Cano

de

Calle

Convento
San Vicente

Fernandez

Gregorio
Marañón

CALLE DE MIGUEL

Calle

General Álvarez de Castro

Santísima Trinidad

Garcia

Paredes

**Museo
Sorolla**

Calle

de

Calle

Viriato

Glorieta
Emilio
Castelar

de

Calle Feijoo

Sinagoga

Glorieta
Pintor
Sorolla

PASEO GENERAL MARTÍNEZ CAMPOS

ALMAGRO

ANGEL

TRAFALGAR

CALLE ELOY GONZALO

Iglesia

Calle Sagunto

Convento Esclavas
del Sagrado Corazón

de

Rafael

Fortuny

Calvo

Glorieta
de Quevedo

Calle del

Jordán

Calle
Santa Feliciana

Plaza
de
Olavide

Calle de Raimundo
Lulio

Garcilaso

PASEO DE

EDUARDO

DATO

Glorieta
Rubén
Darío

Pte Enrique
de la Mata
Gorostizaga

Cardenal

Trafalgar

Museo de
Escultura
Abstracta

Rubén
Darío

**Museo
Escultura
Aire Lib**

CALLE DE SAN BERNARDO

Calle Olid

Calle de Palafox

CALLE

DE

LUCHANA

SANTA

Calle del

General Arrando

Calle Jenner

Calle

Monteleón

Calle de Sandoval

Cisneros

Calle Manuel Silvela

San José
de la Montaña

Calle de Caracas

ENGRACIA

Monasterio
Convento
Visitación
Santa María

Esquinza

Calle Marqués
Riscal

**Paseo de la
Castellana**

CALLE CARRANZA

Bilbao

Glorieta
de
Bilbao

Manuela

Calle
Malasaña

CALLE

DE

FUENCARRAL

Calle de Churruca

Calle de Luna

Calle de Nicasio Gallego

Carbonero

SAGASTA

Calle de Zurbarán

MONTE

Calle Fernando El Santo

PASEO DE LA CASTELLANA

CALLE

Calle

Andrés

DE

Calle del

Divino Pastor

SAN

MATEO

Plaza
Alonso
Martínez

Calle de Mejía Lequerica

Calle Serrano Anguita

Alonso
Martínez

**Plaza de
Dos de Mayo**

Calle

de

la

Palma

Jardines

Museo Arquel Riv

Calle Beneficencia

**Museo
Romántico**

Campoamor

de

Calle

Orellana

Colón

Calle

San

Vicente Ferrer

Tribunal

Calle San Lorenzo

JUSTICIA

Calle Fernando

Calle General Castaños

Plaza
de Colón

Calle San

Espíritu

Calle del Tesoro

Calle Marqués de Santa Ana

Calle Jesús del Valle

de la Madera

Santo

Santa

Calle Santa Brígida

HORTALEZA

Pelayo

Calle Belén

Palacio
de
Justicia

Calle Marqués de Ensenada

Museo
de Cera

Biblioteca
Nacional

Calle San Antonio

SAN

Calle Bárbara de Braganza

**Museo
Arqueológic
Nacional**

Convento
de San
Plácido

**Iglesia de
San Antón**

DE

Calle

Calle de Piamonte

Calle de Villanueva

**ESTACIÓN
DE RECOLETOS**

**San Antonio
Alemanes**

Calle del Barco

Calle de Valverde

Calle correo

Calle de Fuencarral

Calle de Augusto Figueroa

Gravina

Chueca

PASEO DE RECOLETOS

Calle del Almirante

**Santa
Bárbara**

Barquillo

Calle de Piamonte

Palacio Marquis
de Salamanca

Calle de Prim

0   250 m

Marcos

Calle de

Plaza
del Rey

**Casa de las
Siete Chimeneas**

de

las

Infantas

Palacio de
Buenavista

Banco de
España

0   250 yds

F   **G**   **H**

2

3

4

5

6

7

Museo Lázaro Galdiano

HIGHLIGHTS

● *The Virgin of Charity*, Caravaggio
● *Landscape*, Gainsborough
● *Saint John in Patmos*, Bosch
● *Portrait of Saskia van Uylendorch*, Rembrandt
● *Luis de Góngora*, Velázquez
● *The Adoration of the Magi*, El Greco

TIP

● Take one of the free guided tours on Sat or Sun at 11.30.

There cannot be many museums like this wonderful oddity, which is surprisingly unfamiliar to many *madrileños*. Every time you go there is something new to discover in this dazzling collection.

A noble art collector José Lázaro Galdiano, an obsessive, seemingly unfocused art collector who died in 1948 at the age of 80, was born into Navarre nobility. He married Paola Florido, an Argentinian who shared his affinity for art, and together they devoted their lives to travelling the world in search of treasures. An essentially private man, Galdiano never revealed how much he paid for any of the masterpieces. On his death, he donated his collection to the state, and the museum opened in 1951. Now completely reorganized, the exhibition begins on the ground floor

Portrait of a Lady *by Thomas Gainsborough* (left); The Crusaders before Jerusalem *by Velázquez (right)*

with an assessment of Lázaro's role as patron and collector and displays a representative sample of the collection, which includes paintings by Hieronymus Bosch, Bartolomé Murillo, Rembrandt, Francisco Zurbarán, El Greco, Velázquez, José de Ribera, Turner and Goya, as well as exquisite gold and silverwork, enamelwork, bronzes, medieval stained glass, jewellery, fans and weaponry.

Parque Florido The collection is housed in the Parque Florido, a neo-Renaissance *palazzo* named after Lázaro's wife. The beautifully restored interiors provide a magnificent setting for the treasures on exhibition. Don't miss the spectacular painted ceilings, commissioned specially by Lázaro to decorate what were orginally the family's private apartments. This is the finest of Madrid's smaller art galleries.

THE BASICS

www.flg.es

✚ J4

✉ Serrano 122

☎ 91 561 60 84

🕐 Wed–Mon 10–4.30

Ⓜ Nuñez de Balboa/Rubén Dario, Gregorio Marañón

🚌 12, 16, 19, 51, 89

💶 Moderate, free Sun for EU citizens

♿ Good

Museo Sorolla

- *La Bata Rosa* (Room II)
- *Self Portrait* (Room III)
- *Clotilde en traje de noche* (Room III)
- *Clotilde en traje gris* (Room III)
- Turkish bed, used by Sorolla for siestas (Room III)
- *La Siesta* (Room IV)
- *Las Velas* (Room IV)
- *Nadadores* (Room V)
- *Madre* (Room VI)
- New York gouaches (Drawings Room)

TIP

- On Wednesday, the museum is open all day, right through lunchtime. The lovely gardens are a peaceful spot in bustling Madrid.

This serene spot belonged to Spain's finest Impressionist, Valencian Joaquín Sorolla, who wanted to create an oasis of peace for himself in a busy city. It is the best of Madrid's house museums.

Entrance and gardens The Sorolla Museum is one of the few places in the city to give us a sense of the shape of an artist's life and work. Built in 1910–11 by Enrique María de Repollés, it was the Madrid home of Joaquín Sorolla (1863–1923) and became a museum after Sorolla's widow, Clotilde, donated it to the state. It was opened to the public in 1932. The two small gardens, designed by Sorolla himself as a setting for his collection of fountains and fonts, are a bit of Andalucía in Madrid. The first is an imitation of a part of the Seville *alcázar*, while the second is

Statues in the beautiful gardens of Museo Sorolla (left and right)

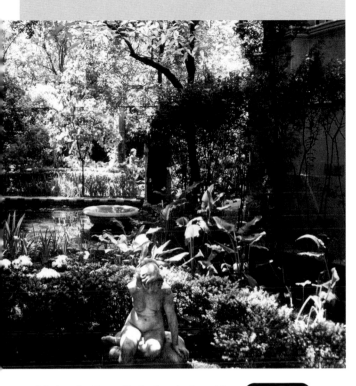

modelled on the Generalife Gardens in Granada's Alhambra. Near the entrance is a replica of a white marble bust of Sorolla by Mariano Benlliure, and to the left is an Andalucian patio.

Inside Lovingly preserved, the house is redolent with turn-of-the-20th-century elegance. The ground floor, with its salon and dining room, gives a real feeling of the artist's life and displays his collection of antique pottery. The upper floor has been converted into a gallery, each room given over to a different aspect of Sorolla's work. Be sure to visit his studio, complete with a Turkish bed for the afternoon siesta. Among the paintings here are several of his wife, Clotilde. Although some see a fairy-tale, picture-postcard quality in his art, there is no denying the brilliance of his handling of light.

THE BASICS

http://museosorolla.
mcu.es
⊞ H4
✉ Paseo del General
Martínez Campos 37
☎ 91 310 15 84
🕐 Tue, Thu, Sat 9.30–3,
Wed 9.30–6, Sun, public
hols 10–3
Ⓜ Iglesia, Rubén Darío,
Gregorio Marañón
🚌 5, 7, 16, 40, 61, 147
💲 Inexpensive. Free
under 18, over 65, Sun
♿ Few

More to See

BOTERO STATUES

In 1994, a section of Castellana was devoted to an exhibition of sculptures by 20th-century sculptor, Fernando Botero. When the exhibition ended, *madrileños* retained a *Hand* in the middle of Castellana; the *Reclining Woman* in Calle Génova; and *Man on a Mule* in the Plaza de Colón.

➕ G/H3 ✉ Plaza de San Juan de la Cruz 🚇 Colón, Nuevos Ministerios 🚌 7, 14, 27, 40, 147, 150

CASA DE LAS SIETE CHIMENEAS

Legend has it that Philip II built the House of the Seven Chimneys in the 1580s for one of his mistresses, who is said to haunt it. During restoration, a woman's skeleton was discovered with coins nearby from Philip II's time.

➕ G7 ✉ Plaza del Rey 🚇 Banco de España 🚌 1, 2, 74, 146

FUNDACIÓN JUAN MARCH

www.march.es

One of Europe's most important private art foundations, this is home to around 30 major annual exhibitions. Often among the most interesting to be found in Madrid, these have focused on Picasso, Kandinsky and Matisse.

➕ J5 ✉ Calle Castelló 77/Calle Padilla 36 ☎ 91 435 42 40 🕐 Mon–Sat 11–8, Sun and public hols 10–2. Closed Aug and between exhibitions. Free guided tours Wed 11, 2 and Fri 4.30, 7.30 🚇 Nuñez de Balboa 🚌 29, 52 💵 Free ♿ Very good

IGLESIA DE SAN ANTÓN

Designed by Pedro Ribera and built by Juan de Villanueva, this example of baroque architecture houses a magnificent art collection, highlighted by Goya's *The Last Communion of Saint José de Calasanz*, painted between 1775 and 1780, and architect Ventura Rodríguez's *Dolphins* statue.

➕ G6 ✉ Hortaleza 63 ☎ 91 521 74 73 🚇 Tribunal, Chueca

MUSEO DE LA CIUDAD

The spacious Museum of the City opened in 1992 and is a high-tech equivalent of the Museo Municipal.

Museo de la Ciudad

The museum explains in almost numbing detail the workings of Madrid's roads and rail, telephone and water systems, and there are some attractive scale models and lots of interactive displays. There are often good temporary exhibitions.

➕ K2 ✉ Calle Principe de Vergara 140 ☎ 91 588 65 99 🕐 Tue–Fri 9.30–8, Sat–Sun 10–2 🚇 Cruz del Rayo 🚌 29, 52 🎫 Free ❓ Guided tours can be arranged in advance ♿ Excellent

MUSEO DE ESCULTURA AL AIRE LIBRE

Connecting the calles Juan Bravo and Eduardo Dato is a road bridge over the Paseo de la Castellana. Underneath is an open-air display of sculpture by many of Spain's best-known contemporary artists.

➕ H4 ✉ Paseo de la Castellana 41 🚇 Rubén Darío 🚌 5, 14, 27, 37, 45

MUSEO ROMÁNTICO

www.museoromantico.mcu.es

This monument to faded romantic glory, founded in 1924, is inside a typical mid-18th-century *madrileño* building that was the home of the traveller-painter the Marqués de Véga-Inclán. Though the content—primarily 18th-century art—might be too sentimental for some, there are many items of interest, particularly Alenza's miniature *Satires of Romantic Suicide*, Goya's *Saint Gregory the Great*, and fine Isabelline and Imperial furniture.

➕ G6 ✉ Calle San Mateo 13 ☎ 91 448 10 45/91 448 01 63 🕐 Tue–Sat 9.30–3, Sun and public hols 10–3. Closed Aug 🚇 Tribunal 🚌 21, 37 🎫 Inexpensive; free on Sun ♿ Very good

PASEO DE LA CASTELLANA

Running in an almost straight line from Colón for 6.5km (4 miles) to Plaza de Castilla, the Castellana is one of Madrid's main points of reference and a centre of business and nightlife. It splits the city in two, and many major sights are on or around it.

➕ H5 🚇 Colón, Rubén Darío, Nuevos Ministerios, Lima, Cuzco, Plaza de Castilla 🚌 5, 14, 27, 40, 45, 147, 149, 150

Museo Romántico

PLAZA DE DOS DE MAYO

2 May 1808 is one of the most famous dates in Madrid's history. It was during the French occupation and a 15-year-old girl, Manuela Malasaña, was shot by French soldiers for smuggling a weapon—a pair of scissors. Earlier in the day, two locals, Velarde and Daoiz, led an attack on the Monteléon artillery barracks (on the site of the present Dos de Mayo square) to capture arms. The insurgency was quashed, but sparked a four-year-long struggle for independence. The area is called Malasaña in memory of the heroine; the square bears the date of the revolt; and the arch in the middle of the square was the gate to the barracks. The dramatic statue here honours the two soldiers who died leading the uprising. Today, the square is lined with small bars and restaurants. Each year, on 2 May, one of Madrid's most popular annual festivals commemorates that fateful day, starting with parades and ending with a classical concert.

🚇 F5 🚇 Bilbao

SALA DEL CANAL DE ISABEL II

Considered one of Madrid's finest examples of industrial architecture, this display space, built in neo-Mudéjar style between 1907 and 1911, mounts frequent excellent photographic exhibitions.

🚇 F3 ✉ Calle Santa Engracia 125 ☎ 91 445 10 00 🕐 Tue–Sat 11–2, 5–8.30, Sun and public hols 11–2 🚇 Ríos Rosas 🚌 3, 37, 149 🖐 Free

SANTA BÁRBARA (LAS SALESAS REALES)

Probably the grandest, if not the most attractive, of Madrid's churches, Las Salesas was commissioned by Bárbara de Braganza, the wife of Fernando VI. It has an elaborate façade built between 1750 and 1758 by Carlier and Moradillo, and contains Sabatini's tomb of Fernando VI (1713–59). The adjoining monastery is currently the home of the Palacio de Justicia, or Supreme Court.

🚇 G6 ✉ Calle del General Castaños 2 ☎ 91 319 48 11 🕐 Daily 5–7pm; and for Mass 🚇 Alonso Martínez, Colón

Paseo de la Castellana (▷ 89)

A Walk North from Sol

Backstreets and boulevards, an arts centre and the up-and-coming area of Malasaña: all are part of this walk.

DISTANCE: 4.6km (2.8 miles)   **ALLOW:** 3 hours

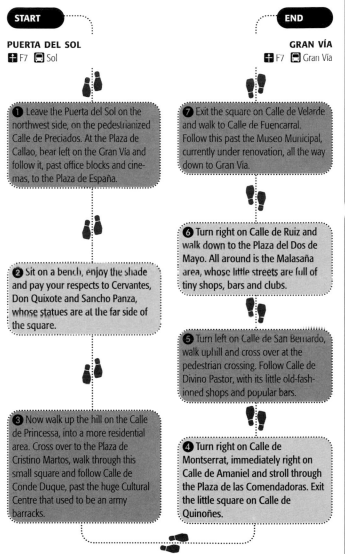

START

PUERTA DEL SOL
✛ F7 🚇 Sol

END

GRAN VÍA
✛ F7 🚇 Gran Vía

1 Leave the Puerta del Sol on the northwest side, on the pedestrianized Calle de Preciados. At the Plaza de Callao, bear left on the Gran Vía and follow it, past office blocks and cinemas, to the Plaza de España.

2 Sit on a bench, enjoy the shade and pay your respects to Cervantes, Don Quixote and Sancho Panza, whose statues are at the far side of the square.

3 Now walk up the hill on the Calle de Princessa, into a more residential area. Cross over to the Plaza de Cristino Martos, walk through this small square and follow Calle de Conde Duque, past the huge Cultural Centre that used to be an army barracks.

7 Exit the square on Calle de Velarde and walk to Calle de Fuencarral. Follow this past the Museo Municipal, currently under renovation, all the way down to Gran Vía.

6 Turn right on Calle de Ruiz and walk down to the Plaza del Dos de Mayo. All around is the Malasaña area, whose little streets are full of tiny shops, bars and clubs.

5 Turn left on Calle de San Bernardo, walk uphill and cross over at the pedestrian crossing. Follow Calle de Divino Pastor, with its little old-fashioned shops and popular bars.

4 Turn right on Calle de Montserrat, immediately right on Calle de Amaniel and stroll through the Plaza de las Comendadoras. Exit the little square on Calle de Quiñones.

Shopping

ABC SERRANO SHOPPING CENTRE

www.abcserrano.com
The tiled exterior of what were the ABC newspaper offices now hide an Aladdin's cave of boutiques. With over 60 to choose from, this is a place to relax and check out the baby clothes and wine, the high fashion and fun jewellery. Good restaurants on site.

✚ H4/5 ✉ Calle de Serrano 61/Castellana 34 ☎ 91 577 50 31 Ⓜ Rubén Dario, Nuñez de Balboa, Serrano

CACAO SAMPAKA

www.cacaosampaka.com
This could be Madrid's most tempting shop. Sampaka sells bars of chocolate as other shops sell silk ties. But it is not just bars. There are books and biscuits, jars and moulds, drinking chocolate and decorations. And the bar-cum-tasting room serves chocolate drinks, mousses, pastries and desserts.

✚ H6 ✉ Calle de Orellana 4 ☎ 91 319 58 40 Ⓜ Alonso Martínez

HOMELESS

www.homeless.es
This boutique was founded in 1994 in San Sebastian as a fundraising venture for the homeless. It now has its own label, 'HOSS'. The designs are casual, but stylish, aimed mainly at young professionals. There's another branch in the Salamanca district (Calle Serrano 16).

✚ F6/7 ✉ Calle Fuencarral 16 ☎ 91 524 17 28 Ⓜ Gran Via

IOLI

Leather shoes and bags, silk hats and purses, all in vivid colours, all designed and made by Cynthia Ioli, the Argentine owner of this tiny shop. Women's shoes can be made to measure.

✚ F6 ✉ Calle del Espiritu Santo 1 ☎ 91 521 00 22 Ⓜ Tribunal

MERCADO DE FUENCARRAL

www.mdf.es
Three floors and an outside area dedicated to the youth market. If you are looking for something out of the ordinary in

NEW MADRID FASHION

Though not yet Paris, Rome, London or even Barcelona, Madrid is slowly gaining a foothold in the world of men's and women's fashion. The international success of Adolfo Domínguez has been followed by that of Roberto Verino, and together with the avant-garde designs of Agatha Ruiz de la Prada and Jesús del Pozo, the Spanish designers are proving a serious threat to more established Italians. The *beau monde* does much of its shopping in the *barrio* Salamanca.

fashion, leisure and culture, this is it: live DJs, hairdressers, tattoo parlours and loads of clothing, jewellery and gifts.

✚ F6 ✉ Calle de Fuencarral 45 ☎ 91 521 41 52 Ⓜ Tribunal, Chueca

PURIFICACIÓN GARCÍA

The sleek look, one of the trademarks of this distinguished Spanish designer of prêt-à-porter men's and women's clothing, is reflected in the minimalist layout of the store.

✚ E8 ✉ Calle de Serrano 28 and 92 ☎ 91 435 80 13/576 72 76 Ⓜ Serrano

RESERVA Y CATA

Don't miss this *bodega* (wine store) in a Chueca basement, offering 600 different wines of mainly Spanish origin.

✚ G6 ✉ Calle de Conde de Xiquena 13 ☎ 91 319 04 01 Ⓜ Colón

SOLAR

Despite Madrid's youth-oriented fashion craze, there are still traditional crafts. For over 50 years, Javier Rojo Solar has been making superb guitars and other stringed instruments at his shop-cum-workshop. Maestros such as Narciso Yepes have been his customers.

✚ F5 ✉ Calle del Divino Pastor 22 ☎ 91 445 72 19 Ⓜ Bilbao, San Bernardo

Entertainment and Nightlife

BAR CAFÉ DEL FORO
Though it does mount straight rock, the Café del Foro also has salsa, fusion and cabaret. Friendly and buzzing venue.
➕ F5 ✉ Calle San Andrés 38 ☎ 91 445 37 52 🚇 Bilbao

BLUE NOTE
This café bar has been reinvented several times over the decades, but is currently known for its jazz and bossa nova, its *mojitos* and *caprinhas*. Opens late and stays open even later.
➕ F6 ✉ Calle de La Palma 11 ☎ 697 340 719
🕐 10.30pm–2am
🚇 Tribunal

CAFÉ MANUELA
After being wowed by the décor, visitors usually find the congenial atmosphere here well suited to writing postcards or chatting to friends. Occasional live entertainment—music concerts, poetry readings, exhibitions by local artists.
➕ F6 ✉ San Vincente Ferrer 29 ☎ 91 531 70 37
🚇 Tribunal

CAFÉ LA PALMA
A cross between a conventional café, a wine bar, a Moroccan tea shop and a nightclub. The music in La Palma is just as eclectic too—everything from rock 'n' roll to flamenco and Cuban fusion.
➕ F6 ✉ Calle de la Palma 62 ☎ 91 522 50 31 🕐 Daily from 4pm 🚇 Noviciado

CAFÉ RUIZ
A relatively peaceful retreat from the night-time mayhem of surrounding Malasaña, the Ruiz retains a late 19th-century feel and serves cocktails as well as coffee and milkshakes.
➕ F5 ✉ Calle Ruiz 11 ☎ 91 446 12 32 🚇 Bilbao

EL CLANDESTINO
Close to the Plaza de Chueca, this may look like just another small night club, but it has a reputation for showcasing great bands for its live music, usually jazz.
➕ G6 ✉ Calle del Barquillo 43 ☎ 91 523 31 06
🕐 11pm–3am 🚇 Chueca

DEL DIEGO
Del Diego's superb design and highly attentive bar staff have quickly made it one of Madrid's big three *coctelerías*, along with El Chicote and

---

CHUPITO
Don't be surprised if, at the end of a meal in a restaurant, your waiter offers you a *chupito*. Usually served in a shot glass, a *chupito* is small but strong: *orujo de hierbas* (a yellow or green herb liquor), *ponche caballero* (spiced orange brandy), *pacharán* (sloe gin). This is on the house, helps to digest the meal and sends you on your way in a happy frame of mind.

Le Cock, two minutes away. This is the place to be or be seen.
➕ G7 ✉ Calle de la Reina 12 ☎ 91 523 31 06
🚇 Gran Vía

EMPIRE
The Empire has five bars on two floors: from above you look down on the people dancing. The age range is 25 to 35.
➕ H6 ✉ Paseo de Recoletos 16 ☎ 91 431 54 27
🚇 Colón

FORTUNY
Glitzy nightclub where you might bump into media celebrities. The terrace garden is the best feature of this former palace, which also has a reputable restaurant. Strict dress code.
➕ H4 ✉ Fortuny 34 ☎ 91 319 05 88 🚫 Closed lunch Sat–Sun in winter 🚇 Bilbao

OJALÁ AWARENESS CLUB
A typical example of the café clubs in Malasaña, this is fun upstairs (movies projected onto walls) and even more fun downstairs, where sand on the floor re-creates summer beach parties, complete with low seats and cushions. Drinks and snacks all day; dinner in the evening.
➕ F6 ✉ Calle de San Andrés 1 ☎ 91 523 27 47
🕐 11am–midnight, later at weekends 🚇 Noviciado, Tribunal

Restaurants

PRICES

Prices are approximate, based on a 3-course meal for one person.
€€€ over €45
€€ €25–€45
€ under €25

EL 4 DE TAPAS (€)
www.4detapas.com
A mix of bar and restaurant in Chueca, this is the place for a crowd that cannot make up its mind: from tapas, salads and peppers stuffed with *bacalao* to pasta and grilled meat, the menu has something for everyone. The setting is modern, with music.
➕ G7 ✉ Calle de Barbieri 4 ☎ 91 523 94 64 🕐 Daily 🚇 Chueca, Gran Vía

BAJO CERO (€)
Madrid has gone mad for an Argentine ice-cream parlour (Bajo Cero means Below Zero), with a design-conscious, lounge-like setting. Order the Giangrossi hand-made ice cream or a pastry, then settle in with your laptop.
➕ F4 ✉ Glorieta Quevedo 6 ☎ 91 445 38 27 🕐 Mon–Thu 8–midnight, Fri 8–2am, Sat 10–2am, Sun 10–midnight 🚇 Quevedo

BAZTÁN (€)
Using the latest vacuum techniques, Paco Rey serves top-class wines by the glass. An ideal spot to learn more about Spain's best wines, this is a new bar in an old *taberna*, overlooking the historic Plaza del Dos de Mayo. Tapas and other well-prepared snacks.
➕ F5 ✉ Calle de San Andrés 14 ☎ 91 523 25 73 🕐 noon–midnight, later at weekends 🚇 Tribunal, Bilbao

NINA MADRID (€€)
With bare brick walls, this is Madrid's answer to the New York look. Always busy, still fashionable, Nina's chefs create Mediterranean-style dishes using seasonal herbs and vegetables, with top-quality fish and meat. Solid Spanish wine list. The weekend brunch (12.30 to 5.30pm) is a social occasion.

APERITIFS

When in Rome…aperitifs still whet the appetite in Spain. Try *vermut* (vermouth), often served on draft from a barrel in many tapas bars. Particularly popular before lunch, vermouth is made from wine infused with herbs and makes an excellent accompaniment for tapas. Order a *vermut con sifón*, with soda, for a refreshing long drink. Sherry is the other great aperitif: *fino* (pale and dry), *manzanilla* (also dry), *amontillado* (a rich, nutty, mature *fino*), *palo cortado* (a rare sherry, between dry and medium), and *oloroso* (rich, but can be dry or sweet).

➕ F5 ✉ Calle de Manuela Malasaña 10 ☎ 91 591 00 46 🕐 Daily 🚇 Bilbao

PEDRO LARUMBE (€€€)
On the top floor of the ABC Serrano, this restaurant is theatrical and luxurious, ideal for that special occasion. Well-known chef Pedro Larumbe uses lobster and asparagus, foie gras and duck for the well-heeled clientele who live nearby. Well-priced wines.
➕ H4/5 ✉ Calle de Serrano 61, 4th floor ☎ 91 575 11 12 🕐 Closed Sat lunch, Sun 🚇 Rubén Dario, Nuñez de Balboa, Serrano

EL PLACER DEL ESPÍRITU SANTO (€)
Typical of the new breed of Spanish cooking, this is a small buzzy restaurant where traditional dishes are given a modern twist: pumpkin ravioli with a tomato and mint sauce, beef cheeks with vanilla, feather-light tiramisu.
➕ F6 ✉ Calle del Espíritu Santo 3 ☎ 91 360 45 16 🕐 Closed Sun dinner, Mon 🚇 Tribunal

LA SACRISTÍA (€–€€)
Popular with local actors and directors, this restaurant is known for its *bacalao* (cod) dishes. It also serves excellent steaks and *gambas* flamed in whisky.
➕ G7 ✉ Calle de las Infantas 28 ☎ 91 522 09 45 🕐 Closed Sun 🚇 Gran Vía

To the north of the downtown are two of the city's great stadiums, the bullring and Real Madrid football club's Bernabéu Stadium. And within an hour or so of Madrid are some of the most historic and beautiful cities in Spain.

Estación
de Chamartín

**Puerta de Europa
(Torres Kio)**

TETUÁN

**Real Madrid
Estadio Santiago
Bernabéu**

CHAMARTIN

AVENIDA DE LA PAZ

**Aquópolis San
Fernando de Henares,
Caprichos Alameda** →

AVENIDA DE AMÉRICA

Aeroporto de
Madrid-Barajas

M30

CHAMBERÍ

PASEO DE LA CASTELLANA

**Plaza
de Toros**

M110

SALAMANCA

PASEO DE LA CASTELLANA

**Fuente
del Berro**

*Parque Quinta
Fuente del Berro*

MADRID

M23

CENTRO

*Parque
del
Retiro*

RETIRO

AVENIDA DE LA PAZ

M30

Faunia

A3/E901

AVENIDA DEL
MEDITERRÁNEO

Estación
de Atocha

ARGANZUELA

*Parque
Cerro
del
Tío Pío*

M30

*Parque
Enrique
Tierno
Galvan*

M30

M203

**PUENTE
VALLECAS**

USERA

A4/E05

**Warner Bros
Park**
↙

Estación
Entrevías

Plaza de Toros

TOP 25

*Plaza de Toros (left);
spectators watching a
bull fight (right); a
matador (opposite)*

THE BASICS

www.las-ventas.com

⊕ M5

✉ Avenida de los Toreros,
Calle Alcalá 237

☎ Museum 91 725 18 57;
Stadium 91 356 22 00

◷ Museo Taurino:
Mar–Oct Tue–Fri 9.30–2.30,
Sun, public hols 10–1,
Nov–Feb Mon–Fri 9.30–2.30

Ⓜ Ventas

🚌 12, 21, 38, 106, 110, 146

Ⓜ Museo Taurino free

❓ Take a 30-min tour of
the bullring, Tue–Sun 10–2.
English spoken €2

♿ None

HIGHLIGHTS

● Bullfighting costumes in
the museum – 'suits of lights'
may contain 5kg (11 pounds)
of gold embroidery
● A papal bull in the
museum (1567) which bans
bullfighting
● *Portrait of Joaquín de
Rodrigo,* attributed to Goya
● Highlight of the season is
in May, during the Feria San
Isidro, when some 30 bullfights take place

**Is bullfighting art or blood sport?
Whatever your feelings, you cannot help
but be impressed by the world's most
important bullring, the place in which a
bullfighter must triumph if he is to
achieve international recognition.**

History and architecture The 1930s bullring is
Madrid's finest example of neo-Mudéjar architecture, a style that resurfaced during the 19th century in imitation of the Mudéjar architecture of the
13th and 14th centuries and is defined by an
interesting use of brickwork and attractive, bright
ceramic tile inlay. In the square in front of the bullring is a melodramatic statue in memory of bullfighter José Cubero, inscribed with the words 'a
bullfighter died, and an angel was born.'

Museo Taurino Half an hour in the stuffy Museo
Taurino next to the stables gives you a basic
overview of the famous names in bullfighting, if
not of the complex art of bullfighting itself. Massive
heads of legendary bulls and portraits of great
bullfighters line the walls, and there are several
dramatic portrayals of bull-runs, including a
notable one by Mariano Benlliure (1868–1947).
The highlights are the *trajes de luces* (suits of
lights), as they are known, among them one
belonging to Juanita Cruz, an early-20th-century
woman bullfighter who was never allowed to fight
on Spanish soil, and another worn by Manolete,
perhaps the greatest of them all, who died in the
ring in 1947. The museum displays are labelled in
both Spanish and English.

FARTHER AFIELD ★ TOP 25

Real Madrid

El Estadio Santiago Bernabéu is Real Madrid's home ground

THE BASICS

www.realmadrid.com

🚦 H1

✉ Calle Conche Espina 1

☎ Stadium: 91 398 43 00; tickets: 902 324 324

🕐 Guided tours in English from Gate 7, Mon–Sat 10–7, Sun, public hols 10.30–6.30. No tours 5 hours before match. Sala de Trofeos Tue–Sun 10.30–7.30, closed 3 hours before match

🍴 Café on site

🚇 Santiago Bernabéu

🚌 14, 43, 120

💷 Tour expensive, trophy room moderate

♿ Good

Founded in 1902, 'Real'—or Royal—rose to become one of the world's most famous football clubs. Its impressive achievements were officially recognized by FIFA, the world governing body, in 1988, when it was awarded the accolade, 'the best club in the history of football'.

El Estadio Santiago Bernabéu Real Madrid have their home in the Santiago Bernabéu stadium. The stadium was inaugurated as the Estadio Chamartín (after the old stadium) in 1947, but the name was changed in 1955 in honour of the club's president. Today it holds more than 80,000 spectators, although before UEFA ruled that all standing places had to be converted to seats it held well over 100,000. In 1982, the stadium had perhaps its greatest hour, when it hosted the World Cup Final (when Italy beat Germany 3–1).

HIGHLIGHTS

● The massive world-famous stadium

● The Trophy Room with its World and European silverware

● The new Realcafé Bernabéu with its views

● Any home match with passionate fans

● The club shop with its array of replica shirts

● The stadium tour

Museum Even if you can't get to a game, you can take a guided tour of the stadium. You will get to enjoy a panoramic view of the inside of the stadium, the pitch and players' tunnel, the away dressing room and the trophy room. Unsurprisingly, given the club's illustrious history, this is packed with silver trophies. Numerous video screens show clips from great matches of the past, including *los blancos*' record nine European Cup triumphs between 1956 and 2006, as well as 17 Spanish cups and 30 Spanish League championships. Success is not limited to football: Real participates in many sports, notably basketball.

AQUÓPOLIS

Spanish children beg their parents to take them to Aquópolis, the biggest and best of the Madrid water parks and one of the largest in Europe. There are huge water slides, an adventure lake and wave machines. There is another Aquópolis, at San Fernando de Henares, 15km (9 miles) east of Madrid. There are rides, a lake and plenty of trees for shade.

🚻 Off map ✉ Villanueva de la Cañada. Carretera de El Escorial km25 ☎ 91 815 69 33 ⏰ Jun, Sep 12–7; Jul–Aug 12–8 🍴 Cafés 🖐 Expensive

At San Fernando de Henares: 🚻 Off map ✉ Carretera Nacional II ☎ 91 673 10 13 ⏰ Jun, Sep 12–7; Jul–Aug 12–8 🖐 Expensive

LOS CAPRICHOS DE ALAMEDA DE OSUNA

This is the closest Madrid comes to a formal English garden. Though a fair distance from the centre, it is pleasant for Sunday strolls.

🚻 Off map ✉ Paseo de la Alameda de Osuna 🚇 Canillejas

FAUNIA

www.faunia.es

Europe's only theme park dedicated to nature and biodiversity. The eight pavilions, each of which re-creates a different ecosystem with the authentic sights, sounds, smells, flora and fauna, will amaze and delight. Experience a tropical rain storm and find out what it's like to live in the Arctic.

🚻 Off map ✉ Avenida de las Comunidades 28 ☎ 91 301 62 35 ⏰ Open daily from 10am; hours vary according to season and day of week. Check 🍴 Cafés 🚇 Valdebernardo 🖐 Expensive

FUENTE DEL BERRO

This intricate little 17th-century garden, just south of the bullring and unfortunately close to the M30 motorway, is a well-kept secret. The attractive Berro fountain is surrounded by lush greenery. There is plenty of welcome shade in summer and several eye-catching statues.

🚻 M6 ✉ Alcalde Sainz de Baranda 🚇 O'Donnell 🚌 15

Waterpark fun

PALACIO REAL DE EL PARDO

www.patrimonionacional.es

Set in a vast park northwest of the city, this former royal palace is usually referred to as El Pardo, after the hill where it stands. Originally a hunting lodge back in 1405, the palace was built for Carlos I and expanded by Carlos III and his architect, Sabatini, in the 18th century. Today, you can visit rooms decorated with fine tapestries designed by Goya and woven at the Real Fábrica de Tapices (▷ 77), as well as murals by Maella and Bayeu. However, many Spaniards are still intrigued to see where General Franco made his home for 35 years. Not to be confused with the nearby Palacio de la Zarzuela, the home of the Spanish royal family since 1962 (not open to the public).

✚ Off map ✉ Calle Manuel Alonso, El Pardo ☎ 91 376 15 00 🕐 Winter: Mon–Sat 10.30–5. Sun, public hols 9.55–1.40. Summer: Mon–Sat 10.30–6pm. Sun, hols 9.25–1.40pm 🍴 Restaurants nearby 💷 Moderate, free Wed EU citizens 🚌 Línea Interurbana 601

By car 14km (8.5 miles) from central Madrid via the M-30, M-605

PUERTA DE EUROPA (TORRES KIO)

These striking towers are named after the Kuwaiti Investment Office, which withdrew funding halfway through construction. The walls are angled inwards at 15 degrees—more than that and they would collapse.

✚ Off map ✉ Plaza de Castilla 🚇 Plaza de Castilla 🚌 5, 27, 42, 124, 125, 147, 149

WARNER BROS PARK

www.warnerbrospark.com

This huge theme park on the outskirts of Madrid opened in 2003. The five zones are all themed: Cartoon Village, Hollywood Boulevard, the Wild West, Super Heroes and Warner Studios.

✚ Off map ✉ San Martín de La Vega. NIV to km22, then M-506 and follow signs ☎ 91 821 1234 🕐 Winter weekends, public hols 12–7; Spring, autumn weekends, public hols 11–8; summer daily 11–11. Days, hours vary, always check 🍴 Cafés, restaurants 🚆 C3 from Atocha 💷 Expensive

Puerta de Europa (Torres Kio)

Excursions

EL ESCORIAL

Philip II's vast palace and monastery was built between 1563 and 1584 as his mausoleum. Apart from its political pedigree, it's also an architectural triumph, with impressive collections of objects and antiques.

The palace contains 16 courtyards, 2,673 windows, 1,200 doors and 86 staircases; 900m (2,952ft) of frescoes line the walls. Its power is breathtaking, and the clear mountain air has left its granite and blue roof slates looking extraordinarily new. Among the highlights are the monastery, the library and the mausoleum, the resting place of most Spanish monarchs since Charles V (1500–58).

THE BASICS

www.patrimonionacional.es
Distance: 60km (37 miles)
Journey time: 1 hour
☎ 91 890 59 02/03
🕐 Apr–Sept Tue–Sun 10–6; Oct–Mar 10–5 (last admission 1 hour before closing)
🚆 Regular trains from Atocha
🎫 Expensive €9 with guide, €7 without guide. Free Wed for EU citizens

SEGOVIA

Segovia, perched on a lofty, rocky outcrop, was founded during the Iberian period and taken by the Romans in 80BC. Occupied by the Moors, it then reverted to the Christians in 1085, and now, a millennium later, is a popular weekend destination for *madrileños* in search of fresh air and a traditional suckling pig lunch.

The first thing you will see is the Roman aqueduct (1st and 2nd centuries AD), with 165 arches and a total length of 814m (2,670ft). In the old town are the magnificent 16th-century cathedral, with its imposing flying buttresses, and the 14th-century Alcázar, or fortress, which was largely rebuilt as a Gothic fantasy in the 19th century and offers lovely views from the top. Segovia is well known as the capital of Castillian cuisine.

THE BASICS

www.segoviaturismo.com
Distance: 88km (55 miles)
Journey time: 2 hours
🚌 La Sepulvedana bus line from Paseo de la Florida 11, near Príncipe Pío Metro station
🚆 From Chamartín station (very slow)
🍴 Candido, Plaza Azoguejo 5
ℹ Plaza Mayor 10 (tel 921 46 03 04); Plaza Azoguejo (tel 921 46 67 20). From Plaza Azoguejo, free guided tours of the city in Spanish (English leaflet) in Jul–Sep. Also, trolley tour (40 mins), daily

TOLEDO

Legendary Toledo, with its hilltop site and fascinating maze of winding streets and hidden patios, one of the nation's most beautiful and legendary cities, was the Spanish capital from 567 to 711, and from 1085 to 1561. In other words, it has played a decisive role in Spanish history for far longer than Madrid.

National Monument Between the 12th and 15th centuries, Moors, Jews and Christians lived there side by side, and its rich combination of Moorish, Christian and Jewish heritage inspired its designation as a National Monument. Highlights are the 13th-century cathedral, the synagogues, Santo Tomé, the Museo de la Santa Cruz (for El Greco paintings) and the Alcázar, founded in 1085.

Alcázar Every culture that has ruled Toledo built a fortress on this site, and all dominated the city's skyline, as does the present-day version. This rather austere fortress was built by Charles V in the 16th century. During the Civil War, owing to its strategic position, it endured a very destructive 70-day siege, and today it houses an army museum that concentrates on those dark days.

Catedral Toledo's cathedral, one of the world's finest Gothic buildings, took 267 years to erect (1226–1493). Among its treasures are a baroque marble, jasper and bronze altarpiece, and paintings by El Greco and Goya.

Judería Although only two of Toledo's original 10 synagogues stand today, there is still a surprising amount to see in the Jewish Quarter. The 14th-century Sinagoga del Tránsito, housing the Museo Sefardí, has a superb Mudéjar interior.

THE BASICS

www.toledoweb.org
Distance: 70km (45 miles)
Journey time: 1 hour 15 mins

🚌 Galeano International from Estación Sur, Méndez Álvaro

🚆 From Atocha, several every hour in summer, less frequent in winter. To avoid a steep climb take a bus up the hill

🛈 Puerta Bisagra (tel 925 22 08 43). Open Mon–Fri 9–6, Sat 9–7, Sun, public hols 9–3. Ride the Zocotren tourist trolley for a 50-min tour of the old town. Leaves from Plaza Zocodover

www.aranjuez.com
Distance: 50km (31 miles)
Journey time: 1 hour
🚌 Estación Sur, Méndez
Álvaro (tel 914 68 22 00)
🚉 Atocha (tel 90 224 02
02)
ℹ️ Plaza de San Antonio
(tel 91 891 04 27). Open
Tue–Sun 10–2, 4–6 (sum-
mer); 10–1, 3–5 (winter)

Palacio Real
☎ 91 891 07 40
🕐 Daily 10–6.15 (sum-
mer); 10–5.15 (winter)
Closed Mon
💰 Moderate; free Wed for
EU citizens

❓ A special Strawberry
Train (Tren de la Fresa) runs
on weekends from Madrid,
from late April through
June. The train departs
Atocha train station at 10.05,
arriving in Aranjuez at 11;
the return journey departs
around 6pm. The ticket
price includes a guided visit
of the palace and gardens,
as well as bowl of straw-
berries en route (tel 90 222
88 22)

ARANJUEZ

**An hour south of Madrid is a city known
as much for a piece of classical guitar
music as for its glorious royal palace. On
the banks of the Tajo River, Aranjuez is
green, leafy and cool.**

Palacio Real This lush landscape inspired Joaquín
Rodrigo (1901–99) to compose the romantic
and hugely popular *Concierto de Aranjuez*. (He
is buried in the town cemetery.) The setting also
drew Spanish rulers from the heat of Madrid.
Although Felipe II commissioned the first palace
back in 1561, the Palacio Real de Aranjuez
took ages to finish: what you see is from the
18th century. But this fairy-tale palace was well
worth the wait, from the throne room with its red
velvet to the gala dining hall with its impressive
chandeliers, furniture, tapestries and sculptures.
One vast room, the Sala de Porcelana, is filled
with porcelain, a particular hobby of Carlos III.
Outstanding works of art include Murillo's
Bautismo de Cristo (*Baptism of Christ*), which
covers the ceiling of the chapel.

Gardens Many gardening enthusiasts go to
Aranjuez just to see the landscaped grounds
around the palace, with their fountains, statues
and walks: the Jardín del Príncipe (Prince's
Garden), the Jardín de Isabel II, the Jardín de la
Isla (the Island) and the Jardín del Parterre,
designed by Boutelou in 1746, with fine cedar
trees, magnolias and flowers.

Strawberries But the whole town is a pleasure to
visit, with its old houses and small palaces, many
of which are still in private hands. The town is also
famous for its strawberries: a day trip to Aranjuez
to eat strawberries is a Madrid tradition.

Where to Stay

On a budget or celebrating a special event? With family or just looking for a fun weekend away? Even if you want to stay right in the throbbing heart of Madrid, there is accommodation for all wallets.

Introduction

Spain's capital has a wealth of hotels, *pensiones* and *hostales*. If you arrive without a booking, there are accommodation services at the airport and main bus and train stations. Many upper-range hotels, geared to business travel, offer reduced rates at weekends and holiday periods, so it's worth asking about reductions.

Location

The main factor to think about is location. The most popular area for visitors is in the heart of the old town (south of Sol between Plaza Mayor and Plaza de Santa Ana); you can walk to many of the main sights from here. Other options include the Recoletos, the Paseo del Prado or Salamanca. If you want to be right in the heart of the nightlife action, Malasaña and Chueca are good bets.

Types of Accommodation

Spanish hotels are classified, regularly inspected and awarded 1 to 5 stars (*estrellas*). *Hostales* are often hard to distinguish from small hotels and can be better value for money. They are graded from 1 to 3 stars; a 3-star *hostal* is generally on a par with a 2-star hotel. *Pensiones* are family-run establishments with simple rooms and shared bathrooms. Sometimes you are expected to take meals here, so check before booking. If you prefer self-catering, you can also hire apartments from about €60 a night; see websites such as gomadrid.com or madridman.com. It's worth paying for a room with air-conditioning; summer temperatures can exceed 40ºC (104ºF).

DISABLED ACCESS

Look for modern hotels if you require better access and specially adapted rooms (www.access-able.com). These range from the well-priced Ibis Centro with two disabled rooms (www.ibis.com) to the luxury InterContinental Madrid (four rooms, www.ichotelsgroup.com). The website www.laterooms.com lists rooms for the disabled. In Spanish, look for the word *minusválido* (disabled).

Budget Hotels

PRICES

Expect to pay up to €100 per night for two in a budget room.

EUROPA

Offering slightly more than the average budget hotel, including hair-dryers and satellite TV. All rooms have private bath.
➕ F7 ✉ Calle del Carmen 4 ☎ 91 521 29 00 Ⓜ Callao

IBIS MADRID CENTRO

www.ibishotel.com
On the site of a famous theatre, this is a practical and friendly 64-room hotel in Malasaña, one of the up-and-coming areas of the city. A good base, with plenty of restaurants and bars nearby. Excellent breakfasts.
➕ F5 ✉ Calle de Manuela Malasaña 6 ☎ 91 448 58 16 Ⓜ Bilbao

OLÉ INTERNATIONAL HOSTEL

www.olehostel.com
This Malasaña hostel (open 24 hours) has a good kitchen, common room with satellite TV and internet, and lockers for valuables. Linen and breakfast are included and towels are available.
➕ F5 ✉ Calle Manuela Malasaña 23, (1st floor) ☎ 91 446 51 65 Ⓜ Bilbao, San Bernardo

HOTEL RESIDENCIA PAZ

Some rooms of this *hostal* on a quiet street overlook a shady courtyard. It's very clean, very efficient and very friendly.
➕ E7 ✉ Calle Flora 4 (2nd floor) ☎ 91 547 30 47 Ⓜ Sol, Ópera

SAN LORENZO

www.hotel-sanlorenzo.com
The Lorenzo is most notable for its soundproof windows. Décor is stylish and rooms comfortable.
➕ G7 ✉ Calle Clavel 8 ☎ 91 521 30 57 Ⓜ Gran Vía

TRAFALGAR

www.bestwesternhoteltrafalgar.com
The Trafalgar, in a residential area north of the centre, is excellent value. All 48 rooms are nicely decorated in modern style and equipped with satellite TV. There's a restaurant, bar and an indoor swimming pool.
➕ F4 ✉ Calle Trafalgar 35 ☎ 91 445 62 00, fax 91 446 64 56 Ⓜ Iglesia

TRYP GRAN VÍA

www.solmelia.com
As the name implies, this is one of the Tryp group's three hotels on the Gran Vía. That makes it ideal for sightseeing and major attractions such as the Puerta del Sol and the Plaza Mayor. All rooms have the standard requirements, such as TV and air-conditioning. 175 rooms including disabled facilities.
➕ F7 ✉ Gran Vía 25 ☎ 91 522 11 21 Ⓜ Gran Vía

TRYP REX

www.solmelia.com
On the Gran Vía, this 145-room hotel is between the Plaza de España and the Plaza Callao, so it is handy for all the major attractions, as well as for strolling through the old streets. 145 rooms; recently renovated. Good access to public transport.
➕ F7 ✉ Gran Vía 43 ☎ 91 547 48 00 Ⓜ Callao

TRYP WASHINGTON

www.solmelia.com
Right on one of the city's main streets, and within walking distance of all the major attractions, this is a practical but busy downtown hotel. Standard old-fashioned building, but rooms are spacious for the price and have soundproofing. There are 115 rooms, including 19 singles.
➕ E6 ✉ Gran Vía 72 ☎ 91 541 72 27 Ⓜ Banco de España

THINGS TO NOTE

It is worth remembering that, at the lower end of the scale, a good *hostal* may be more comfortable than a poor hotel. All the places on this page are *hostales*. Prices can vary according to season.

Mid-Range Hotels

AROSA

www.hotelarosa.com
Very central, the 139-room Arosa has long been popular, particularly with families, and makes an excellent base.
F7 ⊠ Calle de la Salud 21 ☎ 91 532 16 00 Sol, Gran Vía

ASTURIAS

www.cch.es
Convenient to the Puerta del Sol, the 175-room Asturias is close to the main sights and nightlife. Ask for an inside room if you're sensitive to noise.
G7 ⊠ Calle Sevilla 2 ☎ 91 429 66 76 Sevilla

CARLOS V

www.hotelcarlosv.es
The 67-room Carlos V is clean and bright and is next to the Puerto del Sol. If you can get a room on the sixth floor, you will get a balcony.
F7 ⊠ Calle Maestro Victoria 5 ☎ 91 531 41 00 Sol

CONDE DUQUE

www.hotelcondeduque.es
Giving onto an enclosed square, the 143-room Conde Duque is among the more peaceful hotels near the city centre.
F5 ⊠ Plaza del Conde

Valle Suchil 5 ☎ 91 447 70 00 San Bernardo

GREEN EL PRADO

www.pradohotel.com
In this lovely building, within easy reach of the Prado and the Santa Ana district, windows are double-glazed, ensuring a good night's sleep.
G8 ⊠ Calle Prado 11 ☎ 91 369 02 34 Antón Martín, Sevilla

GALIANO RESIDENCIA

www.hotelgaliano.com
In a quiet location, the Galiano's 29 spacious rooms and old-world feel make it one of Madrid's better-kept secrets.
H5/6 ⊠ Calle Alcalá Galiano 6 ☎ 91 319 20 00 Colón

INGLÉS

The clean, 58-room, family-owned Inglés is pleasantly located in a maze of narrow streets within easy reach of many sights. Good value.
G7 ⊠ Calle Echegaray 8 ☎ 91 429 65 51 Sevilla

LAGASCA

www.nh-hotels.com
This 3-star hotel in the heart of the Salamanca district is near the Calle Serrano shops and a host of good restaurants. It was opened in the early 1990s and its 100 rooms are plainly furnished with wooden floors and striking bathrooms. It also has parking.
J5 ⊠ Calle de Lagasca 64 ☎ 91 575 40 06 Velázquez, Serrano

MEDIODÍA

www.mediodiahotel.com
Opposite Atocha train station, the Mediodía is close to the Reina Sofía and the Prado, and is well connected by public transport. Rooms are spacious and simple and have private bathrooms.
H9 ⊠ Plaza Emperador Carlos V 8 ☎ 91 527 30 60 Atocha

MODERNO

www.hotel-moderno.com
This 3-star hotel is only moments away from the Plaza Mayor and the Puerta del Sol, and has particularly welcoming staff. All 97 rooms have air-conditioning and

private bathrooms, and transport to the airport is provided.
⊞ F7 ⊠ Calle del Arenal 2 ☎ 91 531 09 00 Ⓜ Sol

OPERA
www.hotelopera.com
Rather plain-looking hotel but an excellent location near the opera house. All 79 rooms have satellite TV, some with balconies overlooking old Madrid.
⊞ F7 ⊠ Cuesta de Santo Domingo 2 ☎ 91 541 28 00 Ⓜ Ópera

SENATOR GRAN VÍA
www.hotelsenatorgranvia.com
This hotel, in the heart of the city, has an interior that neatly blends functionality and urban style. Guests can expect a CD player, iron, free minibar (nothing stronger than beer), coffee-making equipment, cable TV and bathrobes. There's

also a laundry and internet access.
⊞ F7 ⊠ Gran Vía 21 ☎ 91 531 41 51 Ⓜ Gran Vía

HOTEL T3 TIROL
www.t3tirol.com
A comfortable hotel in the middle of the Argüelles business district. Keen shoppers will find this location convenient, as the El Corte Inglés department store is just opposite; Parque del Oeste is also nearby. Hotel amenities include parking, internet access and car rental facilities.
⊞ D5 ⊠ Calle Marqués de Urquijo 4 ☎ 91 548 19 00 Ⓜ Argüelles

TRYP ALONDRAS
www.solmelia.com
A 3-star, 72-room hotel with well-sized, air-conditioned rooms in the affluent Chamberí area. Popular with business-

people during the week, there are attractive weekend rates for visitors. Useful for the Real Madrid stadium. Parking nearby.
⊞ F3 ⊠ José Abascal 8 ☎ 91 447 40 00 Ⓜ Canal, Alonso Cano, Río Rosas

ZENIT-ABEBA
www.zenithotels.com
This modern 4-star hotel is perfect for shoppers as it is just a stone's throw from Goya and Serrano streets. The décor is functional, but the rooms are spacious and comfortable. The restaurant serves traditional Spanish cuisine and opens for lunch and dinner.
⊞ K4/5 ⊠ Calle de Alcántara 63 ☎ 91 401 16 50 Ⓜ Diego de León

ROOM MATE HOTELS

HOTEL MARIO
www.room-matehoteles.com
This was the first of four jolly, budget-priced hotels in the same Room Mate hotel group. Mario is well-placed, close to the Royal Palace and the Ópera. Fun designs, fun atmosphere.
⊞ E7 ⊠ Calle de Campomanes 4 ☎ 91 548 85 48 Ⓜ Ópera

Other Room Mate Hotels include:

HOTEL ALICIA
www.room-matehoteles.com
What was a 19th-century shoe factory is now a 34-room, designer hideaway on the corner of the Plaza Santa Ana.
⊞ F/G8 ⊠ Calle del Prado 2 ☎ 91 389 60 95 Ⓜ Sol, Antón Martín

HOTEL LAURA
www.room-matehoteles.com
36 stylish rooms, almost on the historic Plaza de las

Descalzas, and close to the Plaza Mayor and more.
⊞ F7 ⊠ Travesía de Trujillos 3 ☎ 91 701 16 70 Ⓜ Callao, Santo Domingo, Ópera

HOTEL OSCAR
www.room-matehoteles.com
In buzzy Chueca, the latest Room Mate hotel opened in 2007.
⊞ G7 ⊠ Plaza Vázquez de Mella 12 ☎ 91 548 85 48 Ⓜ Chueca

Luxury Hotels

CASA DE MADRID

www.casademadrid.com

A short walk from the Royal Palace, this newly opened, exclusive hotel is owned by art historian and interior designer, Marta Medina Muro. Each room is exquisitely decorated and furnished, some with antiques.

➕ E7 ✉ Calle Arrieta 2 ☎ 91 559 57 91 Ⓜ Ópera

HOSPES

www.hospes.es

A new and rather romantic boutique hotel in a classic 1883 building, this is perfectly placed within walking distance of the Prado, the Thyssen-Bornemisza, the Retiro and shopping.

➕ H7 ✉ Plaza de la Independencia 3 ☎ 90 225 42 55 Ⓜ Retiro, Banco de España

INTERCONTINENTAL MADRID

www.madrid.intercontinental.com

Grand and central, with lots of marble and glass, this is where businesspeople, politicians and film stars stay. Rooms and bathrooms are spacious and comfortable. In summer, the courtyard garden restaurant has live music. Popular brunch on Sunday.

Attractive weekend rates.

➕ H4 ✉ Paseo de la Castellana 49 ☎ 91 700 73 00 Ⓜ Gregorio Marañón

ME MADRID REINA VICTORIA

www.mebymelia.com

In the heart of the action, in what was once the formal old Reina Victoria (where bullfighters always stayed) is now Madrid's hip and happening hotel. Expect all the usual luxuries, from 300-thread count linen and down pillow top mattresses to organic, all-natural products for the shower. Stardust is provided by the Midnight Rose restaurant and its owner, Rande Gerber, husband of Cindy Crawford. 192 rooms.

➕ F8 ✉ Plaza de Santa Ana 14 ☎ 91 701 60 00 Ⓜ Anton Martín

HOTEL PUERTA AMÉRICA

www.hotelpuertamerica.com

An excitingly different hotel: 19 architects/designers from 13 countries combined to create this major addition to the city's hotel scene. Expect 12 floors of vibrant colours, with a rooftop bar, black swimming pool and imaginative restaurant. Not central, but close to Serrano shopping.

➕ L3 ✉ Avenida de América 41 ☎ 91 744 54 00 Ⓜ Cartagena

RITZ

www.ritzmadrid.com

Spain's first luxury hotel, opened in 1910 and lives up to its name with 167 luxurious rooms in belle époque style. Between spring and autumn there's a delightful terrace-restaurant.

➕ H7 ✉ Plaza de la Lealtad 5 ☎ 91 901 67 67 Ⓜ Banco de España

HOTEL URBAN

www.derbyhotels.com

Slick and cool, the hard edges of this contemporary city centre retreat next to the Parliament building are softened by original and ancient Oriental, Latin American, African and Egyptian works of art. 96 designer bedrooms with all the latest gadgets; swimming pool. The chic Glass Bar is a popular rendezvous.

➕ G7 ✉ Carrera de San Jerónimo 34 ☎ 91 787 77 70 Ⓜ Sol, Sevilla

Madrid is easy to get to from anywhere in the world. Although very walkable, the city also has excellent public transport. The main thing is to understand the hours when *madrileños* work, eat and play.

Need to Know

Planning Ahead

When to Go

Because of its position high on the inland plateau, Madrid can have some of the most extreme weather conditions in central Spain. Spring, early summer and autumn are the best times to visit. Although tourist crowds dwindle in winter, the weather can be bitterly cold, with temperatures rarely above freezing during the day, and icy after dark.

TIME

Spain is six hours ahead of New York, nine hours ahead of Los Angeles, and one hour ahead of the UK.

AVERAGE DAILY MAXIMUM TEMPERATURES

JAN	FEB	MAR	APR	MAY	JUN	JUL	AUG	SEP	OCT	NOV	DEC
48°F	52°F	59°F	64°F	70°F	79°F	88°F	86°F	77°F	66°F	55°F	48°F
9°C	11°C	15°C	17°C	21°C	26°C	31°C	30°C	25°C	19°C	13°C	9°C

Spring (March to mid-June) vies with autumn as the most pleasant time of year, with clear skies and sunny days, though there may be showers.
Summer (mid-June to August) is hot and dry. Rain is unusual between June and October. July and August are particularly hot.
Autumn (September to October) has little rain, sunny days and moderate temperatures.
Winter (November to February) has dry, clear days and low temperatures.

WHAT'S ON

January *Cabalgata de Reyes* (5 Jan): A procession marks the Three Wise Men's arrival.
San Antón (17 Jan): Pets are blessed in the San Antón Church, Calle Hortaleza 63.
February *Carnival*: A week of processions and parties ends on Ash Wednesday with the ritual 'Burial of the Sardine' by the River Manzanares.
ARCO: International contemporary arts festival.
April *Semana Santa* (Holy Week): Hooded, shoeless, chain-dragging *penitentes* bear images of Christ and the Virgin on their shoulders. On Holy Thursday, during the procession around La Latina, the entire *barrio* takes to the streets.
May *Labour Day* and *Madrid Day* (1–2 May): Concerts region-wide; the main venue is Plaza Mayor.
San Isidro (15 May): Nightly concerts in Plaza Mayor mark the week leading up to the saint's day of San Isidro.
June *San Antonio de la Florida* (13 Jun): Street party marks St. Antonio's feast day.
San Juan (23 Jun): Fireworks in the Retiro to celebrate the festival of St. John.
August *Veranos de la Villa*. Madrid's summer festival of music, dance, theatre and more.
October *Festival de Otoño*: International performing arts festival (through November).
November *International Jazz Festival:* Venues all over the city.
December *Fiestas de Navidad:* Christmas lights, markets and crèches lead up to Christmas. Christmas fair in Plaza Mayor.
New Year's Eve: Thousands gather for the fireworks in the Puerta del Sol.

Madrid Online

www.spain.info
The official website for tourism in Spain, with pages in Spanish, English, German, French, Italian, Japanese and Chinese. Easy to navigate, with plenty of useful information.

www.okspain.org
Aimed at the US market, this has plenty of information, plus details of travel agents and tour operators that are Spain specialists. It also lists all the Spanish tourist offices in the USA.

www.munimadrid.es/www.esmadrid.com
The official site of the Ayuntamiento (city council) has two portals. The traditional look is on www.munimadrid.es; www.esmadrid.com is the newer version, with pages in English, French and other languages.

www.turismomadrid.es
The official site of the Comunidad de Madrid, the autonomous Region of Madrid. In Spanish and English, with pages in other languages, it also covers nearby places such as Segovia, San Lorenzo de El Escorial, Toledo and Aranjuez. Excellent.

www.eldibuk.com
Choose which part of Madrid you want to explore, click on the map and up come listings for everything from restaurants and bars to shops. Fun and funky; designed for locals as well as tourists. Spanish and English.

www.ctm-madrid.es
Come to terms with getting around Madrid by browsing this clear and useful site covering buses and the metro (in English).

http://madrid.lanetro.com
Even a modicum of Spanish will be enough to access probably the best and zappiest of the Spanish-language events and listings sites, covering music, clubs, films and restaurants.

GOOD TRAVEL SITES

www.fodors.com
A complete travel-planning site. You can research prices and weather; book air tickets, cars, and rooms; ask questions (and get answers) from fellow travellers; and find links to other sites.

www.renfe.es/ingles
The official site of Spanish National Railways, with an English-language option.

www.wunderground.com
Good weather forecasting.

CYBERCAFÉS

Café Comercial
🔢 F5 ✉ Gta de Bilbao 7
☎ 91 521 56 55
🕑 Mon–Thu 7.30–1am,
Fri–Sat 8.30–2am, Sun
10–1am 🚇 Bilbao

Ono.com
🔢 F6 ✉ Gran Via 59
☎ 91 448 39 52 🕑 24
hours 🚇 Plaza de España
Also at:
✉ Fuencarral 121
🚇 Alonso Martinez

UFO
🔢 E6 ✉ Princesa 25
☎ 91 547 89 26
🕑 Mon–Fri 9–9 🚇 Ventura
Rodriguez

Getting There

ENTRY REQUIREMENTS

● Anyone entering Spain must have a valid passport (or official identity card for EU nationals). Visa requirements are subject to change, check before making your reservations.

● As of 2007, passengers on all flights to and from Spain have to supply advance passenger information (API) to the Spanish authorities. Full names, nationality, date of birth and travel document details, namely a passport number are required. This information is compulsory. Travel agents should be able to collect this information at the time of booking, or it can be given to staff at check-in desks.

CUSTOMS REGULATIONS

● The limits for non-EU visitors are 200 cigarettes or 50 cigars, or 250g of tobacco; 1 litre of spirits (over 22 per cent) or 2 litres of fortified wine, 2 litres of still wine; 50ml of perfume. Travellers under 18 are not entitled to the tobacco and alcohol allowances.

● The guidelines for EU residents (for personal use) are 800 cigarettes, 200 cigars, 1kg tobacco; 10 litres of spirits (over 22 per cent), 20 litres of aperitifs, 90 litres of wine, of which 60 can be sparkling wine, 110 litres of beer.

AIRPORTS

All flights arrive at Madrid-Barajas Airport, 12km (7.5 miles) northeast of the city. There are four terminals: T1, T2, T3 and the newest, T4, which is used by major international airlines such as Iberia and British Airways. For more information on arrivals and departures from each terminal, go to www.aena.es, ☎ 90 240 47 04.

ARRIVING BY AIR

There are tourist information areas at the airport and leaflets with information about getting to Madrid from Barajas. Terminals T1, T2 and T3 are served by Metro station Aeropuerto (line 8); trains run from 6am to 1.30am. Terminal 4 is linked to the Barajas station (at the end of Line 8) by EMT bus 201, or to the Aeropuerto station with the free AENA (airport) shuttle buses that run between terminals T2, T3 and T4.
A taxi from the airport to the middle of Madrid takes around 30 minutes and costs €20–€25. For more information on ground transport, www.aena.es and www.metromadrid.es.

ARRIVING BY TRAIN

RENFE (www.renfe.es), Spain's national rail company, has two mainline stations in the city. Trains from northern Europe, France and Barcelona (including the high-speed AVE train) arrive on the north side of the city at Chamartín. Trains running to and from Portugal and the south of Spain (including the high-speed AVE train) use Atocha, close to the city centre. RENFE's UK agents are Spanish Rail

(☎ 020 7725 7063, www.spanish-rail.co.uk) or
Freedom Rail (☎ 0870 757 9898; www.free
domrail.co.uk). For more information, also see
www.turismomadrid.es and
www.esmadrid.com.

ARRIVING BY BUS
Madrid is served from other parts of Spain by
many private bus companies. Inter-city coach
services arrive at the Estación Sur de Autobuses
on Calle Méndez Alvaro, southeast of the city
centre. Buses from outside Spain (England,
Portugal and France) also terminate here. For
all bus information ☎ 91 468 42 00.

ARRIVING BY CAR
Drivers access Madrid via the Spanish system of
toll motorways (*autopistas*) or highways
(*autovías*). From France and the north, routes
run along both the Mediterranean and Atlantic
coasts then head towards Madrid; routes
through the Pyrenees are slower but more
scenic. Madrid is clearly signposted at all
interchanges. From southern Spain, take the
A-4 from Seville via Córdoba. From Portugal
take the A-5 from Badajoz. All roads connect
with the three ring roads circling Madrid: the
M30, M40 and M45. Head for Paseo de la
Castellana, Madrid's main artery—most central
locations are easily reached from here.

SENSIBLE PRECAUTIONS
● Carry valuables in a belt, pouch or similar—
not in a pocket. Be especially wary in the
crowds around Plaza Mayor, Puerta del Sol
and the Rastro.
● Do not keep valuables in the front section of
your rucksack. If possible, wear your rucksack
on your front on buses and trains.
● Be aware of street tricks around tourist
attractions. These include distracting you in
conversation, or spraying foam on your back
and then offering to clean it off while some-
one else grabs your bag.

INSURANCE

Check your insurance cover-
age and buy a supplemen-
tary policy if necessary. EU
nationals receive medical
treatment with the EHIC,
European Health Insurance
Card—obtain this form before
travelling. Full health and
travel insurance is still
advised.

**VISITORS WITH
A DISABILITY**

General access in Madrid is
patchy, but gradually improving. For getting around,
buses and taxis are the best
bet, although only the
newest buses have facilities
for people with disabilities.
New buildings and museums
have excellent wheelchair
access, older attractions have
yet to be converted, and
churches are particularly
difficult. English-language
advice is available on
www.access-able.com.
FAMMA is the Spanish
association that deals with
all disabilities (in Spanish
only, www.famma.org).

Getting Around

BUSES

● The bus system is efficient and far-reaching, with regular scheduled services to all parts of the city and its suburbs.

● Finding your way is made easy, as the various routes and stops are shown at every bus stop on a plan.

● There are two types of buses—the standard red bus and the yellow microbus. Both operate between 6am and midnight, and charge €1 for each one-way ride in the city, though the *bono* or Metrobus ticket giving 10 rides costs €6.40 (see below).

● Night buses (known locally as *buhos*, meaning owls) operate from Plaza de Cibeles to many suburbs between midnight and 6am and the tickets cost the same as during the day. The night bus service is not as punctual as the daytime one.

● Bus information offices are located in Plaza de Cibeles and Puerta del Sol, where you can pick up route maps and schedules.

METRO

● The Metro system is very reliable and the best way of getting around the city quickly.

● There are 12 lines, each with a different colour and number shown on route maps and at stations.

● The Metro is constantly expanding and improving. Most of the new stations are on the outskirts of this fast-growing city, built to speed commuters to and from work. Most of all, the Metro is clean and safe for visitors.

● The system is split into zones, with most of it in Zone A, while the outlying areas and lines are in zones B1, B2 and B3.

● A single journey ticket (*sencilla*) within Zone A costs €1 (€1.75 for all zones), but you can get a Metrobus ticket, giving 10 rides, for €6.40

● A tourist card (*abono turistico*) is also available for visitors, and can be for 1, 2, 3, 5 or 7 days. A 1-day pass costs €3.80 for Zone A, a 7-day pass €19.80, with reductions of up to 50 per cent for children. You would need to make six Metro or bus trips a day for it work out cheaper than a Metrobus ticket.

● You can buy tickets (also valid for the buses) from Metro stations in the city and from some newsagents and tobacconists.

● The Metro system runs from 6am to 2am; schedule information and a full Metro map are available from www.metromadrid.es (☎ 902 444 403), or from any station. Also see www.ctm-madrid.es, which has all the information in English as well as Spanish

● Metro trains run about every 3 to 6 minutes from Monday to Friday; this extends to every 15 minutes after midnight, and there are slightly fewer trains on weekends.

● It's best to avoid the rush hours, generally 7–9.30am and 7–9pm, when it gets very busy.

TAXIS

● Official taxis are white with a diagonal red stripe. A green light on the roof shows when they are free.

● The standard base taxi fare is €1.85, with a charge of €0.65 for every further kilometre. There is a supplement payable on Sundays and holidays, and for certain destinations, such as the rail station, airport and bullring.

● Make sure the meter is turned on and set at the base fare for your journey

● The major private taxi companies in Madrid are TeleTaxi (☎ 91 371 21 31), Radio Taxi (☎ 91 447 32 32) and Eurotaxi (☎ 91 540 45 03).

TRAINS

● Chamartín, north of Plaza de Castilla, is the terminus for northern destinations. It is linked by a through line with Atocha.

● *Cercanías* refers to local and suburban trains, *largo recorrido* to intercity and long-distance trains.

GUIDED WALKS

Official guided tours of the city leave regularly from the Madrid Tourism Centre on Plaza Mayor 27. They go on foot, by bus and even by bicycle. There are 12 different themes, such as the Oldest Madrid (Mon, 10am, in English), Great writers (Tue, 10am, English) and 20th-century architecture (Thu, 10am, English). It is important to book ahead at the tourist office or by phoning ☎ 91 588 29 06. Cost is €3.25 per person.

For a really special experience, get under the skin of Madrid on a tour run by the Spanish-American husband and wife team of Carlos and Jennifer Galvin, who run LeTango Tours. They take you to the places that locals go, explaining how various traditions began and why they persist. One of the most entertaining walks is a foodie-oriented 'tapas tour' (☎ 91 522 39 28, mobile 661 752 458, toll free US 1 866 866 5107; www.letango.com).

A British guide with a passion for the Duke of Wellington, Stephen Drake-Jones also runs the Wellington Society, devoted to understanding the history of Spain in general and Madrid in particular (mobile 609 143 203; www.wellsoc.org).

Essential Facts

LOST AND FOUND

● Municipal Lost Property Office (Oficina de Objetos Perdidos) ✉ Paseo del Molino 7 ☎ 91 527 95 90 Ⓜ Legazpi ⏰ Mon–Fri 9–2

● For objects lost on a bus: EMT ✉ Cerro de la Plata 4 ☎ 90 250 78 50 Ⓜ Pacífico ⏰ Mon–Fri 9–2. Ask for *objetos perdidos*.

● To claim insurance, you must obtain a *denuncio* (signed statement of loss) from a police station.

MONEY

The euro (€) is the official currency of Spain. Banknotes are in denominations of 5, 10, 20, 50, 100, 200 and 500 euros, and coins in denominations of 1, 2, 5, 10, 20, 50 cents and 1 and 2 euros.

10 euros

50 euros

200 euros

500 euros

ELECTRICITY

● The standard current is 220 volts.
● Plugs are of the round two-pin type.

ETIQUETTE

● Spaniards rarely form orderly queues, but are generally aware of their place in the service order.

● Though there are clearly marked 'No Smoking' areas in many restaurants, many Spaniards smoke anyway. Smoking on buses and trains is banned.

● Stretching and yawning in public is considered vulgar.

● Do not be worried about using your voice to attract attention in bars and restaurants. Say *Oiga* (Oy-ga, literally 'hear me').

● In restaurants, it can take longer to get the bill than the meal; if you're in a rush ask for the bill when ordering your final course.

● Drinks are normally paid for before you leave the bar, not on a round-by-round basis.

● Tipping is discretionary, but 5 per cent is normal practice.

MONEY MATTERS

● Most major travellers' cheques can be changed at banks. American Express offers the best travellers' cheque rates.

● Credit cards are now accepted in all large establishments and many smaller ones.

● There are many multilingual ATM/cash machines.

OPENING HOURS

● Shops: 9–1.30, 5–8; department stores: 9–9. Some are open Sundays.

● Churches: 9.30–1.30, 5–7.30. Many only open half an hour before a service.

● Museums: many close on Mondays.

● Banks: Mon–Fri 9–2; between October and May many banks open from 9–1 on Saturdays.

MAIL

● Buy stamps (*sellos*) from post office

(*oficina de Correos*) or tobacconists (*tabac*), indicated by a yellow and brown sign.

● Madrid's most central post office is ✉ Plaza de Cibeles ☎ 91 396 27 33 🕐 Mon–Fri 8.30am–9.30pm, Sat 8.30–2. The post office at Mariano Fernández 1 is open seven days a week: weekdays 8.30–10pm, Sat 9.30-10pm, Sun and hols 12–10pm (☎ 91 459 50 29).

● Post boxes are yellow with two slots, one marked 'Madrid' and the other for everywhere else (marked *Provincias y extranjero*).

TELEPHONES

● Public telephones take €1 and €2 coins and 2c, 5c, 10c, 20c and 50c coins.

● Phone cards are available from newsstands; some phones accept credit cards.

● The technology for mobile, or cell, phones in Spain is GSM, which may be incompatible with some countries, for example, the USA or Japan. Tri-band mobiles/cell phones will work. Check to make sure your phone will work and what the cost of calls will be. Charges for roaming, using your phone in another country, can be high.

● To call Spain from the UK dial 00 34 followed by 91 for Madrid and then the seven digit number. To call the UK from Spain dial 00 44. To call Australia dial 00 61. To call South Africa dial 00 27.

● To call Spain from the US dial 011 34 followed by 91 for Madrid and then the seven digit number. To call the US from Spain dial 001.

MEDICINES AND HEALTHCARE

● Pharmacies (*farmacias*) are indicated by a flashing green cross; they are usually open 9.30–2 and 5–8. All post a list of *farmacias de guardia* (all-night chemists) and highlight the closest ones.

● Madrid's pharmacists are often happy to let you have some prescription medicines without a prescription.

EMERGENCY NUMBERS

● Police (Local) ☎ 092
● Police (National) ☎ 091
● Police (Guardia Civil) ☎ 062
● Police, Ambulance, Fire ☎ 112
● Fire station: Madrid ☎ 080
● SATE is a special 24-hour service for foreign tourists who need to report crimes to the police. In Spanish, English and French ☎ 90 210 21 12; www.es.madrid.com.

TOILETS

Gone are the days when tourists needed to worry about hygiene in toilets in restaurants and bars. Modern Spain has modern toilet facilities.

TOURIST OFFICES

Plaza Mayor 27 ☎ 91 588 16 36 🕐 9.30–8.30

Calle del Duque de Medinaceli 2 ☎ 91 429 49 51 🕐 Mon–Sat, 8–8; Sun, hols 9–2.

Estación de Atocha ☎ 91 528 46 30 🕐 Mon–Sat 8–8; Sun, hols 9–2.

Estación de Chamartín ☎ 91 315 99 76 🕐 Mon–Sat 8–8; Sun, hols 9–2pm.

Madrid-Barajas Airport Terminal 1 ☎ 91 305 86 56 🕐 Mon–Sat 8–8; Sun, hols 9–2.

Terminal 4 ☎ 90 210 00 07 🕐 Mon–Sat 8–8; Sun, hols 9–2.

Language

English is now the second language of many, if not most, Europeans. Staff in Madrid's hotels, many restaurants and even many shops speak English. However, it is fun to try a few words in Spanish and, of course, any efforts are appreciated! In bars, the tapas on offer are often chalked up on a board.

PRONUNCIATION

c before an *e* or an *i*, and *z* are like *th* in thin
c in other cases is like *c* in cat
g before an *e* or an *i*, and *j* are a guttural sound which does not exist in English—rather like the *ch* in loch
g in other cases is like *g* in get
h is normally silent
ll is similar to y
y is like the *i* in onion
Use the formal *usted* when speaking to strangers; the informal *tu* for friends or younger people.

COURTESIES	
good morning	*buenos días*
good afternoon/evening	*buenas tardes*
good night	*buenas noches*
hello (informal)	*hola*
goodbye (informal)	*hasta luego/hasta pronto*
hello (answering the phone)	*¿Diga?*
goodbye	*adios*
please	*por favor*
thank you	*gracias*
you're welcome	*de nada*
how are you? (formal)	*¿Como está?*
how are you? (informal)	*¿Que tal?*
I'm fine	*estoy bien*
I'm sorry	*lo siento*
excuse me (in a bar)	*oiga*
excuse me (in a crowd)	*perdón*

USEFUL WORDS	
I don't know	*No lo sé*
I don't think so	*Creo que no*
I think so	*Creo que sí*
It doesn't matter	*No importa*
Where?	*¿Dónde?*
When?	*¿Cuándo?*
Why?	*¿Por qué?*
What?	*¿Qué?*
Who?	*¿Quién?*
How?	*¿Cómo?*
How much/ many?	*¿Cuánto / cuántos?*
Is/are there?	*¿Hay?*
ticket	*entrada*

BASIC VOCABULARY

yes/no	sí/no
I do not understand	no entiendo
left/right	izquierda/derecha
entrance/exit	entrada/salida
open/closed	abierto/cerrado
good/bad	bueno/malo
big/small	grande/pequeño
with/without	con/sin
more/less	más/menos
hot/cold	caliente/frío
early/late	temprano/tarde
here/there	aquí/allí
today/tomorrow	hoy/mañana
yesterday	ayer
how much is it?	¿cuánto es?
where is the...?	¿dónde está...?
do you have...?	¿tiene...?
I'd like.....	me gustaría...
I don't speak Spanish	no hablo español

FOOD

apple	manzana
banana	plátano
beans	habas
chicken	pollo
clams	almejas
duck	pato
fish/seafood	pescado/marisco
fruit	fruta
lamb	cordero
lettuce	lechuga
lobster	langosta
meat	carne
melon	melón
orange	naranja
pork	cerdo
shrimp	gambas
squid	calamare
tomato	tomate
tuna	atún
turkey	pavo

RESTAURANT

smoking allowed	se permite fumar
no smoking	se prohibe fumar
menu	la carta
fork	tenedor
knife	cuchillo
spoon	cuchara
napkin	servilleta
glass of wine	copa
glass of beer	caña
water (mineral)	agua (mineral)
still	sin gas
sparkling/bubbles	con gas
coffee (with milk)	café (con leche)
May I have the bill/check	¿La cuenta, por favor?
Do you take credit cards?	¿Aceptan tarjetas de crédito?
tavern	mesón/taberna
cakes	pasteles
small snacks	pinchos
sandwiches	bocadillos
set dishes	platos combinados

SHOPPING

ATM/cash machine	Cajero
I want to buy...	Quiero comprar...
belt	cinturón
blouse	blusa
dress	vestido
shirt	camisa
shoes	zapatas
skirt	falda
tie	corbata
small	pequeño
medium	mediano
large	grande
cotton	algodón
silk	seda
wool	lana
café	cafetería
breakfast	desayuno
lunch	almuerzo
dinner	cena

Timeline

NEED TO KNOW TIMELINE

BEFORE AD800

Iberian tribes inhabited Madrid from around 1000BC. The Romans ruled the Iberian peninsula between 218BC and the 5th century AD and Madrid became a stopping place.

In AD711, Muslims defeated the Visigoths—areas of Spain came under Muslim rule for 800 years.

854 Muhammad I of Córdoba founds the city of Madrid.

1083 Madrid is recaptured by Alfonso VI; Christians, Jews and Muslims all inhabit the city.

1202 Alfonso VIII recognizes Madrid as a city by giving it Royal Statutes.

1309 The Cortes, or Parliament, meets in Madrid for the first time.

1469 The marriage of Catholic monarchs Ferdinand and Isabella unites Aragon and Castile.

1492 The conquest of Granada completes the unification of Spain. Spain begins a 200-year period of imperial power, and expels the Jews.

1561 Philip II establishes Court in Madrid: a cultural 'Golden Age' begins.

1578 Philip III (1598–1621) is the first monarch to be born in Madrid.

1617–19 Plaza Mayor is built.

1759 Charles III begins a modernization schedule for Madrid.

1808–12 French occupation; famine kills 30,000. Spanish rule restored 1814.

Below, from left to right: The interview of Columbus with Queen Isabella; Ferdinand the Catholic; Philip II; statue of Philip III in the Plaza Mayor; General Francisco Franco; statue of the painter Goya

1819 Prado museum opens; houses are numbered and streets are named.

1851 The Madrid–Aranjuez railway line is inaugurated.

1873 The Republic is declared.

1917 Spain faces a general strike.

1919 The first metro line in Madrid opens.

1931 The Second Republic is declared.

1936–39 The Spanish Civil War takes place, sparked by uprising in North Africa. The Nationalists win, and the long dictatorship of General Franco follows.

1975 General Franco dies; King Juan Carlos is declared his successor.

1977 The first democratic general election.

1986 Spain joins the EEC (now EU).

1992 Madrid is European City of Culture.

2002 Spain adopts the euro; a landmark in the move to mainstream Europe.

2007 Madrid becomes the world's third largest Metro system after London and New York, with over 300km (186 miles) of lines.

MADRID PEOPLE

Charles III
Charles III is often known as 'the best mayor that Madrid ever had'. More than any other single historical figure, he is responsible for today's Madrid. He came to the throne in 1759 and was a keen proponent of Enlightenment ideals.

Cervantes
Cervantes is the author of *Don Quixote*, believed by some to be the first novel ever written. A tax collector, he wrote *Don Quixote* while in jail for manipulating accounts. He died in Madrid in 1616.

Goya
Goya (1746–1828) is the painter most readily associated with Madrid, though he neither was born nor died here. He settled in Madrid in 1774 and became Court painter to Charles IV in 1789.

NEED TO KNOW TIMELINE

GOYA

Index

Madrid's
25 Best

WRITTEN BY Jonathan Holland
ADDITIONAL WRITING Paul Wade and Kathy Arnold
DESIGN CONCEPT AND DESIGN WORK Kate Harling
COVER DESIGN Tigist Getachew
INDEXER Marie Lorimer
IMAGE RETOUCHING AND REPRO Michael Moody, Sarah Montgomery and Matt Swann
REVIEWING EDITOR Jacinta O'Halloran
SERIES EDITOR Paul Mitchell

ISBN 978-1-4000-1879-6

FOURTH EDITION

IMPORTANT TIP
Time inevitably brings changes, so always confirm prices, travel facts, and other perishable information when it matters. Although Fodor's cannot accept responsibility for errors, you can use this guide in the confidence that we have taken every care to ensure its accuracy.

SPECIAL SALES
This book is available for special discounts for bulk purchases for sales promotions or premiums. Special editions, including personalized covers, excerpts of existing books, and corporate imprints, can be created in large quantities for special needs. For more information, write to Special Markets/Premium Sales, 1745 Broadway, MD 6–2, New York, NY 10019 or email specialmarkets@randomhouse.com.

Colour separation by Keenes
Printed and bound by Leo, China
10 9 8 7 6 5 4 3 2 1

A03144
Maps in this title produced from mapping © MAIRDUMONT / Falk Verlag 2007
Transport map © Communicarta Ltd, UK

The Automobile Association wishes to thank the following photographers, companies and picture libraries for their assistance in the preparation of this book.

Abbreviations for the picture credits are as follows – (t) top; (b) bottom; (l) left; (r) right; (c) centre; (AA) AA World Travel Library.

1 AA/R Strange; 2 AA/M Jourdan; 3 AA/M Jourdan; 4t AA/M Jourdan; 4c AA/M Jourdan; 5t AA/M Jourdan; 5c AA/M Jourdan; 6t AA/M Jourdan; 6cl AA/R Strange; 6cr AA/M Chaplow; 6bl AA/M Chaplow; 6bc AA/M Jourdan; 6br AA/S Day; 7t AA/M Jourdan; 7cl AA/M Jourdan; 7cr AA/C Sawyer; 7bl AA/M Chaplow; 7br AA/M Jourdan; 8 AA/M Jourdan; 9 AA/M Jourdan; 10t AA/M Jourdan; 10ct AA/M Jourdan; 10c AAM Chaplow; 10cb AA/M Jourdan; 10/11 AA/M Jourdan; 11t AA/M Jourdan; 11ct AA/M Jourdan; 11c AA/R Strange; 11cb AA/M Chaplow; 12t AA/M Jourdan; 12b AA/R Strange; 13t AA/M Jourdan; 13ct AA/M Jourdan; 13c AA/M Jourdan; 13cb AA/M Jourdan; 13b AA/M Jourdan; 14t AA/M Jourdan; 14cr AA/M Jourdan; 14c AA/M Chaplow; 14cb AA/M Jourdan; 14b AA/M Chaplow; 15t AA/M Jourdan; 15b AA/M Chaplow; 16t AA/M Jourdan; 16ct AA/M Chaplow; 16c AA/M Jourdan; 16cb AA/M Chaplow; 16b AA/J Edmanson; 17t AA/M Jourdan; 17ct AA/M Jourdan; 17c AA/M Chaplow; 17cb AA/M Chaplow; 17b AA/J A Tims; 18t AA/M Jourdan; 18ct AA/M Chaplow; 18c AA/C Sawyer; 18cb Photodisc; 18b Brand X Pictures; 19(i) AA/M Jourdan; 19(ii) AA/M Jourdan; 19(iii) AA/M Jourdan; 19(iv) AA/R Strange; 19(v) AA/M Chaplow; 20/21 AA/M Jourdan; 24l AA/M Chaplow; 24r AA/M Chaplow; 25l AA/R Strange; 25c AA/R Strange; 25r AA/M Jourdan; 26l AA/M Chaplow; 26r AA/R Strange; 27l AA/M Chaplow; 27r AA/P Enticknap; 28 Museo Cerralbo; 28/29 Museo Cerralbo; 30l AA/R Strange; 30r AA/R Strange; 31l Museo Traje; 31r Museo Traje; 32 AA/M Jourdan; 32/33t AA/M Jourdan; 32/33b AA/M Jourdan; 33t AA/M Chaplow; 33cl AA/M Jourdan; 33cr AA/M Jourdan; 34l AA/R Strange; 34r AA/R Strange; 35l AA/M Chaplow; 35c AA/M Chaplow; 35r AA/M Chaplow; 36t AA/M Jourdan; 36b AA/M Jourdan; 37t AA/M Jourdan; 37b AA/M Jourdan; 38 AA/M Jourdan; 39 AA/R Strange; 40 AA/M Jourdan; 41 Imagestate; 42 Imagestate; 43 AA/R Strange; 46 AA/M Jourdan; 47l AA/M Jourdan; 47c AA/M Chaplow; 47r AA/M Jourdan; 48 AA/M Chaplow; 48/49 AA/M Jourdan; 50l AA/R Strange; 50r AA/M Chaplow; 51l AA/M Jourdan; 51c AA/M Jourdan; 51r AA/M Chaplow; 51l AA/M Jourdan; 52c AA/M Chaplow; 52r AA/M Chaplow; 53l AA/M Jourdan; 53r AA/M Jourdan; 54l The Vision of St. Alphonsus Rodriguez (1533–1617), Zurbarán, Francisco de (1598–1664), Real Academia de Bellas Artes de San Fernando, Madrid, Spain, Bridgeman Art Library; 54/55 Alamy (Alex Segre); 56t AA/M Jourdan; 56b AA/M Jourdan; 57t AA/M Jourdan; 57bl AA/M Chaplow; 57br AA/M Chaplow; 58t AA/M Jourdan; 58bl AA/M Chaplow; 58br AA/M Chaplow; 59t AA/M Jourdan; 59bl AA/J Edmanson; 59br AA/M Jourdan; 60 AA/M Jourdan; 61 AA/R Strange; 62 AA/R Strange; 63 AA/M Jourdan; 64 AA/M Jourdan; 65 Imagestate; 66 Imagestate; 67 AA/J Edmanson; 70l AA/M Jourdan; 70/71t AA/M Jourdan; 70c AA/M Jourdan; 70/71c AA/M Jourdan; 71t AA/M Jourdan; 71cl AA/M Jourdan; 71cr AA/M Jourdan; 72 AA/M Jourdan; 73l AA/M Chaplow; 73r AA/M Chaplow; 73r AA/M Chaplow; 74l AA/M Jourdan; 74r AA/M Jourdan; 75l AA/R Strange; 75r AA/J Edmanson; 76t AA/M Jourdan; 76bl AA/M Chaplow; 76br AA/M Chaplow; 77t AA/M Jourdan; 77b AA/M Jourdan; 78 AA/R Strange; 79t AA/M Jourdan; 79c Imagestate; 80 Imagestate; 81 AA/R Strange; 84 Alamy (INTERFOTO Pressebildagentur); 84/85 The Crusaders before Jerusalem (oil on canvas), Velázquez, Eugenio Lucas (1817–70), Museo Lazaro Galdiano, Madrid, Spain, Bridgeman Art Library; 86 AA/M Chaplow; 86/87 AA/R Strange; 88t AA/M Jourdan; 88c Museo de la Cuidad; 89t AA/M Jourdan; 89b AA/M Chaplow; 90t AA/M Jourdan; 90b AA/R Strange; 91 AA/M Jourdan; 92 AA/R Strange; 93 AA/M Jourdan; 94 Imagestate; 95 AA/M Jourdan; 98l AA/M Jourdan; 98r AA/M Jourdan; 99 AA/M Jourdan; 100l AA/M Chaplow; 100r AA/M Chaplow; 101t AA/M Jourdan; 101 AA/C Sawyer; 102t AA/M Jourdan; 102b Alamy (Kevin Foy); 103t AA/M Chaplow; 103lbl AA/M Chaplow; 103bl AA/M Chaplow; 103br AA/M Chaplow; 103rbr AA/M Chaplow; 104 AA/M Chaplow; 105t AA/M Chaplow; 105bl AA/M Chaplow; 105bc AA/M Chaplow; 105br AA/M Chaplow; 106t AA/M Chaplow; 106bl AA/J Edmanson; 106bc AA/J Edmanson; 106br AA/J Edmanson; 107 AA/C Sawyer; 108t AA/C Sawyer; 108ct Photodisc; 108c Photodisc; 108cb Photodisc; 108b Stockbyte; 109 AA/C Sawyer; 110 AA/C Sawyer; 111 AA/C Sawyer; 112 AA/C Sawyer; 113 AA/M Chaplow; 114 AA/M Chaplow; 115 AA/M Chaplow; 116 AA/M Chaplow; 117t AA/M Chaplow; 117b AA/M Chaplow; 118t AA/M Chaplow; 118b AA/R Strange; 119 AA/M Chaplow; 120 AA/M Chaplow; 121 AA/M Chaplow; 122t AA/M Chaplow; 122b AA/M Chaplow; 124t AA/M Chaplow; 124bl AA; 124bc AA; 124br AA; 125t AA/M Jourdan; 125bl AA/M Jourdan; 125bc Illustrated London News; 125r AA/M Jourdan

Every effort has been made to trace the copyright holders, and we apologise in advance for any unintentional omissions or errors. We would be pleased to apply any corrections in any following edition of this publication.